"I have been giving financial advice primarily to couples for the last forty-plus years. I only wish I had had this book forty years ago, as it validated from a research standpoint just about everything that I've experienced in working with couples on their finances. It is a privilege to offer this endorsement."

Ron Blue, CEO, Ron Blue Institute

"Money can be one the greatest sources of tension and conflict in marriage. By uncovering what's really going on beneath the surface, Shaunti and Jeff reveal the actions any couple can take to truly transform their marriage. This book is an amazing resource I'll be using both personally and in ministry."

—Steve Carter, stewardship pastor,
Southeast Christian Church

"Money problems are often not about money, but about how we think and feel about money, ourselves, and our spouse. And we don't often know *why* we think and feel the way we do. Shaunti and Jeff's research is a roadmap to discovering what lies behind our attitudes and behavior around money—and learning to work as a team. I highly recommend *Thriving in Love and Money* for all who want to replace conflict with harmony."

—Gary Chapman, PhD,
author of *The 5 Love Languages*

"You know that money conversation you've been avoiding. There's a reason behind it, and it might surprise you. With X-ray vision and the data to back it up, *Thriving in Love and Money* offers practical insights that will help you get past the relational dynamics that block fiscal fitness. It's a great investment in your 'us' and financial health."

> —Ron L. Deal, bestselling family author,
> speaker, and therapist, coauthor of *The Smart Stepfamily Guide to Financial Planning* and *Building Love Together in Blended Families*

"Jeff and Shaunti Feldhahn have done it again. Their newest research goes right to the core of a huge topic that every couple deals with—money—and *why* we respond the way we do. It is fascinating to suddenly understand our spouse's motivations, wishes, and fears—and our own! No matter how much or how little money we have, this is exactly what we need in order to thrive. Both men and women will love this book!"

> —Dr. Emerson Eggerichs, founder of Love & Respect Ministries and *New York Times* bestselling author of *Love & Respect*

"As marriage coaches, we know that what's going on underneath the surface always fuels what's above the surface. Handling money in marriage is no different. Couples will have so much more harmony once they understand their *thoughts*, *feelings*, and even *fears* about money. Before you develop another budget, take a financial class, or track your spending, READ THIS BOOK. You will be so surprised at what you learn about yourself and your spouse—and how simple it is to have a great relationship around money!"

> —Jill and Mark Savage, founders of Hearts at Home and authors of *No More Perfect Marriages*

"Shaunti and Jeff's skillful integration of research, relational understanding, and practical wisdom make this book a must-read for every couple. The insight and helpful prompts will be a game changer in your relationship!"

—Dr. Juli Slattery, cofounder, president,
Authentic Intimacy

"Shaunti and Jeff have tackled such an important topic for relationships. This is a money book that has nothing to do with money, and everything to do with the heart."

—Lysa TerKeurst, #1 *New York Times* bestselling author
and president of Proverbs 31 Ministries

"In our work with married couples from all over the world, we've found that money issues rank near the top of the list of marriage stressors and causes of divorce. Our friends Jeff and Shaunti Feldhahn have combined their unparalleled expertise with some eye-opening research data to write a book that will undoubtedly help countless couples avoid the common money pitfalls in many marriages. *Thriving in Love and Money* will equip you and your spouse with the tools to simultaneously improve your finances, your communication, and your marriage as a whole. Every couple (including us) would benefit from implementing the truths outlined in this book!"

—Dave and Ashley Willis, authors of *The Naked Marriage*, hosts of *The Naked Marriage Podcast*, and speakers for MarriageToday

thriving
in love and
money

Other Nonfiction Books and Resources by Shaunti Feldhahn and/or Jeff Feldhahn

Thriving in Love and Money Discussion Guide
Thriving in Love and Money Discussion Kit
For Women Only: What You Need to Know
about the Inner Lives of Men
For Men Only: A Straightforward Guide
to the Inner Lives of Women
For Young Men Only: A Guy's Guide to the Alien Gender
(coauthored with Eric Rice)
For Young Women Only: What You Need to Know about How Guys Think
(coauthored with Lisa Rice)
For Parents Only: Getting Inside the Head of Your Kid
(coauthored with Lisa Rice)
3-in-1 For Women Only, For Men Only, For Couples Only DVD Study
Through a Man's Eyes: Helping Women Understand the Visual Nature of Men
(coauthored with Craig Gross)
For Women Only in the Workplace
The Male Factor
The Surprising Secrets of Highly Happy Marriages
The Good News about Marriage (with Tally Whitehead)
The Kindness Challenge
The Life Ready Woman (coauthored with Robert Lewis)
Made to Crave for Young Women (coauthored with Lysa TerKeurst)

Devotionals and Bible Studies by Shaunti Feldhahn

Find Rest: A Women's Devotional for Lasting Peace in a Busy Life
Find Peace: A 40-Day Devotional Journey for Moms
Find Balance: Thriving in a Do-It-All World

Fiction Books by Shaunti Feldhahn

The Veritas Conflict
The Lights on Tenth Street

thriving in love and money

5 Game-Changing Insights
about Your Relationship,
Your Money, and Yourself

Shaunti and Jeff Feldhahn

BETHANYHOUSE
a division of Baker Publishing Group
Minneapolis, Minnesota

© 2020 by Veritas Enterprises, Inc.

Published by Bethany House Publishers
11400 Hampshire Avenue South
Bloomington, Minnesota 55438
www.bethanyhouse.com

Bethany House Publishers is a division of
Baker Publishing Group, Grand Rapids, Michigan

Printed in the United States of America

Library of Congress Cataloging-in-Publication Data
Names: Feldhahn, Shaunti, author. | Feldhahn, Jeff, author.
Title: Thriving in love and money : 5 game-changing insights about your
    relationship, your money, and yourself / Shaunti Feldhahn, Jeff Feldhahn.
Description: Minneapolis, Minnesota : Bethany House Publishers, [2020]
Identifiers: LCCN 2019041330 | ISBN 9780764232558 (cloth) | ISBN
    9781493423026 (ebook)
Subjects: LCSH: Communication in marriage. | Interpersonal communication. |
    Finance, Personal—Decision making. | Money.
Classification: LCC HQ734 .F3733 2020 | DDC 302—dc23
LC record available at https://lccn.loc.gov/2019041330

ISBN 9780764236242 (trade paper)

Cover design by Lucy Iloenyosi, NeatWorks, Inc.

Authors are represented by Calvin W. Edwards.

20   21   22   23   24   25   26   7   6   5   4   3   2   1

Research Team

Left to right: Melinda Verdesca, Suzanne Stewman, Caroline Niziol, Katie Phillips, Jeff Feldhahn, Calvin Edwards, Shaunti Feldhahn, Eileen Kirkland, Charlyn Elliott, and Naomi Duncan. Not pictured: Deanna Hamilton.

Theresa Colquitt

Tally Whitehead

Dr. Charles Cowan, Analytic Focus

Sonali Saxena, Analytic Focus

Michelle Frisella, Dynata

Kin Parikh, Dynata

Mauricia Wills, Decision Analyst

Not pictured: Additional survey professionals at Dynata.

Contents

1 It's Not About the Money

How we woke up to what really matters—
and you can too

I listened in disbelief to the voice on the other end of the phone.

"As you know, money can cause a lot of issues in marriage, but we don't believe it has to. How would you feel about making this your next research study—and us funding it?"

Three thoughts jumped immediately to mind:

Is this a trick question?!

Wow, God, you're amazing!

But then . . .

Oh NO.

You see, money was the last big area where Jeff and I were *not* on the same page. Over the years, as we had investigated and uncovered crucial truths that help relationships thrive, we had absorbed all that knowledge into our own marriage. It had been game-changing.

Except we had never studied money.

And I wasn't sure I wanted to.

But this out-of-the-blue phone call was a pretty strong signal that we were *supposed* to.

Thinking About This Part of Life in a Whole New Way

Before we go further, let's explain what this little book is about, who we are, and the research process that got us here.

Our names are Jeff and Shaunti Feldhahn, and we're going to share what we've discovered about how to thrive when dealing with money in marriage (or any romantic relationship, really). These pages won't focus on the usual technical financial stuff—there are already great resources out there on investment advice, how to create a budget, and the best ways to tackle debt.

Those things are important. But you can make great investments, create a budget, have no debt . . . and still have tension about money! You can still be confused about your spouse's decisions and frustrations—and even your own.

It reminds me (Shaunti) of a recent speaking engagement in Boston. The organizers had a great plan, we were in an excellent facility, and the technical setup seemed perfect. Yet when they turned on my microphone, the sound system would screech or ring. Pretty soon we avoided using my mic and winced when we did, expecting an unpleasant interaction.

It's kind of like that with money. Even when we set all the technical stuff up right, there can be awkwardness or unpleasantness when we have money conversations. So sometimes it's easier to avoid them. But if we don't talk, we won't understand each other. Part of us is hidden from our spouse. Pretty soon, we're simply not thriving in an area that is a big part of daily life—and a big (if sometimes unseen) part of our relationship.

As one thirty-year-old husband exclaimed in a focus group:

> I just want marital financial happiness, you know? There's got to be a path to get there. We've been married six years, and we didn't really talk about money in premarital counseling. Over time we've figured out how to live within our means, which is obviously where budgeting helps. But it doesn't solve the main issue of what we can do to succeed in our *marriage* when it comes to money.

I just want marital financial happiness.

That's honestly what most of us want, isn't it? We just want to thrive in love and money.

It may sometimes seem out of reach. But it's not!

It's Not About the Money

Here's the truth under everything we'll be covering. When we have conflict around money, *it's not about the money*.

Otherwise, on financial issues, rich people would never fight! Instead, it's about things under the surface that we don't even realize are there. How money makes us feel. Insecurities and fears. How we process things—and how our spouse does.

These factors—and what we assume about our spouse in the midst of them—can cause either conflict or connection. They play out in little ways, in our spouses and in ourselves, every day. Often without us seeing what is really going on.

For example, suppose I call Jeff on the way home from a tiring day of meetings to suggest that I get Chinese takeout for the family. He pauses and says, "Well . . . I've got some chicken breasts from Costco in the fridge that I can grill instead. It'd be cheaper to just do that, okay?"

Why does that bug me?!

And similarly, why might it bug him that I call and suggest takeout?

The reasons have very little to do with money. (I promise we'll share the real reasons in a later chapter.)

Five realities under the surface

So if it's not about the money, what is it about? Here are the key discoveries we'll unpack in this book. Below are examples of common thoughts and frustrations around money—and the five things that are really going on.

Our subconscious thoughts	What is really going on
Why can't you see that this is so worth it / so not worth it?	We aren't valuing what our partner values.
Don't you care that I am worried about _____?	We have fears our partner doesn't comprehend and are using money to try to relieve them—which may be making our partner's fears worse.
You're not the boss of me/ I just want to handle money the way I want to handle money.	Subconsciously (or consciously), we are resisting being fully one in marriage—and it is coming out in how we think about and handle money.
You're not listening/what are you *thinking*?	We are clashing instead of connecting due to our different wiring for processing and communication.
It's so obvious why we should/shouldn't do _____. I can't believe you don't agree.	We're having a knee-jerk reaction to something, because of wrong assumptions about money or our spouse.

Our money frustrations with our spouse are actually signals to look deeper, to see the real issues under the surface. Once our eyes are opened, everything changes. We now know *why* our spouse got irritated or reacted to a certain situation in the way they did. We see the reasons for our own feelings and reactions—motivations, expectations, and hot buttons we might not have been able to articulate, even to ourselves. Most important, we can work on solving the *real* issue so the frustrations happen a lot less often.

Money gives us a window into the heart. And as we peer into each other's thoughts, dreams, and fears, we not only resolve or prevent problems, but grow closer than we ever have been before.

> Our money frustrations with our spouse are actually signals to look deeper, to see the real issues under the surface.

That's what we're focusing on in these pages: understanding the often-unseen, day-to-day, money-related factors that impact relationships, so that money ends up being an opportunity for intimacy and connection rather than conflict.

Your tour guides for today . . .

Since we're going to be spending some time together, here's a bit more about us. We live in Atlanta, have two teenage children, and—we're not quite sure how we're old enough for this!—have been married twenty-five years. For more than half of that time we've been investigating the little things that make a big difference in relationships and writing books about them. These have all been based on extensive, nationally representative research studies. This book is the culmination of the tenth such study we have conducted since 2003 (although the book also includes insights from most of the others).

Our background is a bit different. Rather than being PhD psychologists, we both have analysis backgrounds. Both of us received professional graduate degrees from Harvard University (which is where we met).

I (Jeff) am an attorney by training. After getting my JD from Harvard Law School, I spent eight years in corporate law at various firms before branching out as a technology entrepreneur.

I (Shaunti) got a master's in public policy with a concentration in business, then worked on Wall Street as a financial analyst. When Jeff and I moved to Atlanta, I unexpectedly became a bestselling author. That started a completely different path of writing, speaking, and social research, using our analytical experience in a new way.

For simplicity's sake we're going to have me (Shaunti) be the primary voice in these pages, although Jeff will jump in frequently.

The research

Although Jeff and I are the primary researchers, this project relied on an extensive research team. More than twenty professionals were heavily involved, especially our longtime research and survey design consultant, Dr. Charles Cowan, former chief of survey design at the US Census Bureau and the founder and president of Analytic Focus.

During the research process, we investigated one main question: "What is underneath our responses to money in marriage (or romantic partnership), that either does or does not allow us to thrive?" Jeff and I cast a wide net to hear people's money stories, habits, and perspectives, hitting up random contacts like our Uber driver in Dallas, a pregnant couple in Connecticut, a retiring CFO in Edmonton, counselors in Sydney. Organizations in Seattle, Louisville, El Paso, Fredericksburg (Virginia), and San Diego—among other cities—set us up with dozens of confidential in-person interviews and focus groups. I stopped people in grocery stores and on the subway, and walked the aisle of an Airbus on a cross-country flight, buying lunch for whoever would answer some anonymous, written questions.

This effort culminated with the series of rigorous surveys referenced in this book:[1] one special-purpose independent survey, and three nationally representative surveys totaling 1,822 married or cohabiting individuals. The latter three were conducted in partnership with three leading companies: Decision Analyst (which we have used for most of our previous surveys), Dynata, and SSI (which was acquired by Dynata shortly after our survey was conducted).

All told, our conclusions are based on nearly three years of interviews, focus groups, and surveys with more than 3,000 men and women across a diverse array of demographics including age, racial background, religious background, socioeconomic group, orientation, income-earning status, marital status/living situation, and many other factors.[2] (In addition, several topics draw on the accumulated research conducted with more than 20,000 men and women in our nine other nationally representative studies since 2003.) For our methodology, see the online Appendix 1 by Chuck Cowan. You can find comprehensive survey results on our research portal (shaunti.com/research).

All this was made possible by the sponsorship of Thrivent Financial, a large member-owned financial services company that funded 75 percent of our independent research costs. (Thrivent is a not-for-profit, with both a business and missional reason to give back; we are very grateful they are choosing to invest in healthy relationships in an area that has long needed it.)

How to use this book

Having come to terms ourselves with what we have learned from our research, we want to encourage you: Read this book with humility and a willingness to have your eyes opened. If you are reading this so you can point out all the flaws in how your spouse handles finances, it will not help you thrive in love and money! But if you are willing to upend your perceptions about your spouse *and* yourself, it will do wonders for your marriage and money journey. We recommend this book as the first part of a process:

First, you and your spouse highlight what applies to each of you personally and talk about it. We call this the Love and Money Exchange. This alone can dramatically improve your understanding and interactions around money.

Step 1: Read this book with a pen in hand and make notes on what applies to *you personally* and what does not. One of you might use the left margin for "your" notes ("This is exactly how I think," "This is why I got upset when you said XYZ yesterday," "This section isn't really me"), and the other use the right margin. (For convenience, some people actually prefer to each mark up their own copy of the book.)

Step 2: Once each of you has marked it up, go back and read through your partner's notes for a personalized tour of how they think and feel.

Step 3: Take the opportunity to talk it through, hearing more about what your spouse is thinking. For one example of *how* to talk about it, see the "Love and Money Conversation Model" at the back of the book. (More on this in a moment.)

Next, build on what you've learned, identifying and addressing the specific needs and issues in your *relationship.* Either during or after reading the book, we recommend several key resources on our website, thriveinloveandmoney .com, including assessments and several video-driven guides, including the *Thriving in Love and Money Discussion Guide*. You can use these alone, as a couple, or in a small group.

Finally, investigate practical financial resources. You will quickly discover that the practical side of working on finances together becomes much more simple and enjoyable once you understand where each of you is coming from.

At all stages, our website, thriveinloveandmoney.com, will have pointers to key resources we believe will be most simple and helpful.

Let's return to our recommendation that each of you read and make notes on what applies to *you*. There is one big caveat: If you are reading the same copy of the book, someone is going to have to be vulnerable first. For many of us, this will add a temptation for Spouse #1 to censor themselves (because they don't yet know how candid Spouse #2 will be!) and/or for Spouse #2 to read those comments and respond rather than simply reading and noting their own thoughts.

If you think you generally will be able to avoid these temptations, then proceed however you like.

But if one or both of you feels you need space and grace on the topic of money, another option might be to each write "your" notes in a separate notebook and then share your thoughts. Or, as mentioned, even each get your own copy of the book in which to write—and then trade and read your spouse's copy.

What if you are reading the book solo, or your spouse doesn't want to do the Exchange? Still capture what applies to you, but also note "aha" moments or questions about your spouse ("Is this what he/she was feeling yesterday?"); both will help you understand—and perhaps discuss—your and their reactions down the road.

A note for those engaged to be married: Couples who learn these things *before* living together and merging finances can set themselves up well and head off a host of problems. But you also may not always know which dynamics apply to you! (*"I* think *that's how I feel . . . but I'm not sure, since I haven't had to share finances yet."*) That's okay. Make notes where you can, but also capture practical ideas you might want to adopt (as well as dynamics you want to avoid). You can also find resources for engaged couples at our website.

A few caveats

Before we dive in, a few key notes to keep in mind.

There are always exceptions. We have worked to identify the key factors that are true and helpful for most of us. But they won't be representative of everyone. If 80 percent of our respondents said they feel a certain way on a topic, by definition 20 percent did not! Everyone is an individual. Use the research as a starting point to see what factors play out in you and/or your partner.

This book is targeted to marriage but will be helpful to others. Not surprisingly, the most intense application of these factors occurs in marriage. But people of every marital status were included in the research (single, cohabiting, married, remarried, divorced . . .) and many of these findings will be helpful, regardless. Note that we use "spouse," "mate," and "partner" interchangeably.

We are relying on the latest and most prevalent science around gender. Although most of our findings are not at all gender-related, there are a few that clearly correlate to certain differences between men and women. We know there are many questions around gender today ("Is gender just a social construct?"), but this is not the place for that debate. Here, we are starting from the conclusions of the vast majority of scientific studies (including some of our own) that demonstrate both socialized/"nurture" aspects to gender and clear biological/"nature" differences— including brain wiring differences[3] seen even in utero, and emotional factors that are statistically common (although definitely not limited) to each gender.

Our findings will not apply to highly specialized situations. The vast majority of married couples care about each other and, even if they have problems, are not in dire or abusive situations that require professional intervention. Most also understand (even if they don't always adhere to) basic financial principles (like "You're supposed to pay back what you borrow") and are not grossly financially irresponsible. We'll be focusing on this vast majority of "normal" couples. That said, we have also seen some unusual situations: the truck driver who gambled away the family's life savings, the schoolteacher with the pathological addiction to buying expensive handbags, the ultra-controlling spouse who refused to give his wife any money or information about their finances. If you're in such a situation, please immediately reach out to a specialized therapist for counsel and help.

We will be sharing some faith-based perspectives. As social scientists, our research is rigorous across all religious and nonreligious groups. But in addition, we personally come at life from a Christian perspective, and thousands of churches require our books, such as *For Women Only* and *For Men Only*, as part of premarital counseling. This book will likely be used in the same way. But we also respect the fact that some of you will not share our beliefs; we trust you will understand and respect why we bring in certain faith-based perspectives as we go.

Regardless of belief system, where we are in our relationship, or where we fall on the spectrum of agreement with these findings, the goal is the same: to help us better understand and navigate love and money.

So are you ready to dive in?

Remember my screeching microphone at that event in Boston? After twenty minutes of loud and unsuccessful attempts to fix it, the event organizers sought help from the conference center. A technician slipped into the room, looked carefully at a nest of wires and cables, then disconnected and reattached some of them. Problem solved. He smiled at our effusive thanks and shrugged. "Sometimes the wires get crossed. It's pretty simple, really. You just have to know what to look for."

Sometimes, relationally, our wires get crossed. Thankfully, we don't need to keep wincing away from this topic, because uncrossing the wires can be pretty simple.

Let's dive in and learn what to look for. Including why Jeff and I got annoyed with each other about getting Chinese takeout—and maybe why you have too.

2 A Daily Problem, a Simple Solution

Why talk may be cheap—but is also the most valuable thing you can do

We all tend to get sideways with each other about money. In fact, because we hear money is the leading cause of divorce, we tend to believe money is the most serious issue in marriage. But the truth is more nuanced.

Yes, money can be a real cause of strife, but it can also be an opportunity for connection. And it's not because money is more important than any other issue. It's not that money disagreements are more intense, or last the longest, or are the most vocal—it's because money is everywhere.

The first of two reasons why money is so pivotal in marriage is because we interact with money in some way, somehow, every day.

Right now you are interacting with money. You are reading a book, probably using electric lights, maybe sitting on a chair in a house or apartment. All of these things were paid for. Within a few hours, you'll eat or drink something. You'll send a text or post something about this amazing book (had to sneak that in) via a mobile device you paid for, using a connection you pay for. At every step you are—subconsciously or consciously—evaluating whether various things are "worth it." Whether it's better to save this than spend that.

This chair has gotten uncomfortable—it might be time to get a better one.

I'm cold; I should turn up the heat, but gas is expensive.

This connection is slow, but if I get that better data plan, we may not have enough money at the end of the month.

That constant interaction leads to the second reason money is so pivotal in marriage: Since we can't get away from money, *we can't get away from how money makes us feel.*

And if we're living with another human, we can't get away from how money makes them feel. We can't escape the need to process it, think about it, and talk about it with someone who probably has a very different perspective at times.

In a 2007 study by my friend Dr. Scott Stanley at the University of Denver, he and his coauthor Lindsey Einhorn capture this reality. "Money has symbolic potential unlike almost anything else. . . . Money is unique in that no day goes by for any adult when money is not used, thought of, spent, saved, or worried about."[4]

When someone in a focus group brought up the idea that money was the primary reason for divorce, a divorced man shook his head. "No. People don't get divorced over money. They get divorced over what money brings out in them."

Thankfully, although we all share a common problem, we can also find some simple ways to prevent money from pulling us apart—and ensure it brings us together instead.

About This Chapter

Before we go further, we should note that this chapter is very different from the rest of the book. So skip this chapter and start with chapter 3 if you mostly want to understand yourself, your spouse, and what to do to create a great relationship around money. But if you're interested in what we found about the big-picture problems and solutions (the proverbial 30,000-foot view), keep reading!

The Key Factors

Over the years, our research has focused on digging out what we call the "high-leverage" factors in relationships: little things that make a big difference. We look for those areas where a few changes or "aha" moments can create significant improvement.

If this book were just about prospering in *money*, quite a few technical, financial actions would be high-leverage:

- learning how to develop a budget and live within it, so that a couple builds margin

- avoiding consumer debt and getting out of debt, if possible

- having emergency savings, basic insurance coverage, and diversification in investments

- tithing and giving, so a couple lives from a mindset of gratitude and is reminded that all they have isn't theirs anyway

All these technical financial actions are important. But there are already many helpful resources out there (we link to some on thriveinloveandmoney.com) and we won't reinvent those wheels here.

The issue is this: We can do all of those technical things and still have confusion, frustration, tension, or stress in our relationship.

Here's the key: *If you aren't thriving in the "love" part of love and money, it will be difficult to come together enough to do the "money" part well.* It is difficult to create a stable financial foundation without coming together in the relationship. Clearly this works in reverse too: Money troubles can create a relational strain. But as anyone who

32

has survived bankruptcy or financial heartache can attest, if you are close in your relationship you can get through anything financially.

What a Lack of Thriving Looks Like

Many of us believe that most couples "fight" about money. But the truth is sneakier, and something every couple needs to evaluate.

Across all our surveys, we learned that only about half of us ever "fight" about money. But that doesn't mean everyone else is happily skipping to and from weekly budgeting sessions. For more than nine in ten couples, there are other dynamics that get in the way—and some are even more dangerous to the relationship than raised voices and intense disagreements.

For example, in our Dynata survey, our largest survey of 1,030 respondents, of those who *never* fight, 85 percent still experience tensions in the relationship due to money! Overall (including those who fight), 92 percent of couples experienced those money tensions in some way (Chart 2.1). Our other surveys found similar—or even slightly larger—numbers.[5] Note that due to its specialized nature, we use our independent survey of young-married, young-family churchgoers—which we will call the young families survey—as the primary source for analysis of these tensions.[6]

> **Chart 2.1: How Many Fight/Have Tension About Money?**
>
> **92%** experience one or more points of tension
>
> **44%** experience actual fighting
>
> **85%** of those who never fight still experience one or more points of tension
>
> Source: Dynata survey

Money is indeed one of the primary causes of tension and stress in relationships, according to multiple studies,[7] including in-depth research conducted by Dr. Sonya Britt at Kansas State. (In our review of the research, we do not see a definitive answer that money is the *leading* cause of divorce; other factors appear to be just as or more important to that outcome.[8])

So when money causes relational stress—what does that look like? And what helps solve that stress? The answers below are based in large part on extensive statistical wizardry done by Chuck Cowan to answer those exact questions.

Love and money points of tension

We have identified twenty-six distinct negative dynamics that occur among couples because of money—and statistically, all of them are important. Why? Because if you have one, you'll probably have more.

That said, not all money tensions are created equal.

The list below, from the young families survey, is sorted by which love and money tensions appear to be the most dangerous because they are most predictive of having others. (In case any of you are statistics nerds like me [Shaunti], you can see the details at shaunti.com/research.)

As you'll see here, money-related resentment and anger top the list. Only 44 percent of couples experienced this type of resentment in their marriage. But it is the most dangerous of the tensions: Those who had resentment were far more likely to experience many of the other problems than those who simply experienced anxiety or worry over money. (Worry was much more common, but less dangerous to the relationship.)

Note that actual fighting (raised voices, and so on) doesn't make the top five! Resentment, blame/embarrassment, resignation, frustration/irritation, and exhaustion appear to be more dangerous than fighting.

Take a few minutes now and ask yourself: Which dynamics do you experience in your relationship? And are they rare, or do they occur often?

We all have some of them. (Well, 92 percent of us admit we do. I think the 8 percent who say they don't fall into the "liar, liar, pants on fire" cohort.) Just as important: Where are your tensions on the list? All the tensions are important, but the further up the list, the more seriously you need to take them.

1. **Resentment/anger** ("Why do I have to be on a budget when we have plenty of money?" "Why won't he/she realize how tight things are?")

2. **Blaming the other person OR feeling shame or embarrassment yourself** ("They/I shouldn't have bought it.")

3. **Resignation** ("Fine, have it your way. I give up.")

4. **Frustration/irritation/annoyance** ("Why don't you see things the way I see things?")

5. **Exhaustion** ("How many times do we have to have the same conversation?")

6. **Actual fighting/significant arguing/raised voices** or sharp tones

7. **Pride**—one person doesn't want to admit they were wrong.

8. **Martyrdom** ("I'll sacrifice, even if you won't—or because you won't.")

9. **Feeling defensive** ("I'm not wrong." "I shouldn't have to explain myself." "You're not my mom.")

10. **Superiority/derision OR feeling judged/condescended to** ("You don't live in the real world." "I know how to handle money better." "I'm not wasteful like you." "[eye roll] Everything isn't a crisis, we don't really need this right now.")

11. **Checking out/ignorance about the situation** ("I honestly don't care." "Do what you want to do.")

12. **Not on the same page/disagree/two different sets of goals** or values (Example: One spouse thinks "it's just right to save and be strict"; the other thinks "it's just right to have the flexibility to buy lots of small purchases as we need them.")

13. **Entrenchment** (Digging in. Escalation. Repetition of the message. "Fine, if you're digging in your heels, I'll dig in my heels too.")

14. **Disappointment/discontentment** because one person had an expectation that wasn't met. (For example, "You should just know that I needed that." "You should just know that we can't spend that way." "I don't like asking for more money; you should know I need more.")

15. **Hiding receipts or purchases** (because someone doesn't want to feel judged; to avoid fights).

16. **Retaliatory spending** ("You went out for dinner, so I get lunch out." "You hurt me—so I buy something.")

17. **Misalignment/lack of clarity on goals**—stating, "We can't afford it" when actually it is "We may have the money, but we don't have a line item."

18. **Mismatch of impulsive tendency** ("I want to grab that") **versus planning tendency** ("but we didn't plan for that"). (Impulsive person might think, *You're no fun.* Planner thinks, *Well, I have mastery over MY impulses!*)

19. **Not talking about money/avoidance**

20. **Not feeling cared for** ("You're not aware of me/not attentive" "I don't feel prioritized.")

21. **Doing money separately/excluding yourself/excluding one party**

22. **Anxiety/stress/weight/worry**

23. **Fear about losing control**

24. **Unpaid bills** because you weren't communicating/were avoiding

(rank unknown) **Silent treatment/withdrawal**[9]

(rank unknown) **Ignoring agreements/decisions** (e.g., continuing to go out for lunch every day, even after promising to take a lunch instead)

The High-Leverage Solutions

So if those are the tensions that keep us from thriving in love and money, what are the big-picture solutions? Over the course of this three-year project, our research and analysis found that three intertwined actions will ensure those tensions don't occur as often, and will help get us to that marital financial happiness we're looking for.

We need to:

- build cushion for discretionary purchases

- be able to talk about money

- understand what is underneath how we and our partner respond to money

The big issue (and the reason for the rest of this book) is this: *That final action (understanding what is underneath how we and our partner respond to money) is necessary for you to do the first two well.*

Gaining understanding

At a recent faith-based women's convention, after I (Shaunti) had finished speaking, I stopped by the exhibit hall to shop for my daughter's birthday present. One cute clothing boutique booth was run by a husband-and-wife team I'd met at other events over the years. They asked, "So, what's your next research project?"

When I explained, it was clear the topic resonated. Here's what followed:

Her: We need a budget. We should have a better emergency fund. But I keep putting off planning for it. I wish he didn't *let* me put it off, but I guess he's avoiding it too.

Him: Yeah, that's totally fair. I do hesitate. I just don't know how to create a household budget with income that swings so wildly. Sometimes we bring in a *ton* of revenue from these events. Sometimes we drive home with not enough to pay the mortgage. We always seem to get by. God always provides. But how does someone create a budget with that?!

Me: Jeff and I have had the same conversation! Our speaking income is so cyclical. But when we started this research project on money, we realized there *were* places we could get help to figure out the technical stuff. That wasn't the real reason we didn't have a budget.

Him: [Looking a little uncomfortable] Yeah . . . well . . . it's probably not for us either. I just don't know that we can get to a place where we both agree. I have no problem with planning. I do have a problem planning when it means I'll be clashing about money with her.

This couple needed a budget to build up cushion for their household, but first they needed to be able to talk about it. And to do that, they needed to understand why they had difficulty talking about it; to understand what was really going on with each other, under the surface. That was the engine that would drive everything else.

Understanding fuels talking. Then both the understanding and the dialogue fuel the building of a strong financial foundation—including the cushion that truly helps relationships.[10] In other words, the three "high-leverage solutions" mentioned earlier build on one another.

But that understanding of each other is essential to overcoming money tensions and getting us moving first!

Your household income issues and tensions will be different from ours. But most of us can probably complete this sentence:

I struggle with _____ because I don't like to _____.

I (Shaunti) struggle to talk about budgets with Jeff because I don't like compromising on what I want to buy and do.

I (Jeff) avoid being the one to track the bills each month because I don't like focusing on the fact that my entrepreneurial career choices haven't yielded the income to our family that I thought they would.

We sure hope this helps you, because we feel quite vulnerable sharing these not-so-flattering private thoughts! But here's the thing: It took us a while to figure out what those thoughts actually *were*. You may not be able to fill in those blanks yet. We not only don't understand our spouse at times; we sometimes don't understand ourselves.

It may take you a while to recognize thoughts like:

I resent having to take a sack lunch every day while my wife eats out, because I assume she cares more about her convenience than mine.

I feel un-cared for when I think my husband doesn't want me to have a financial say in things now that he earns all the money.

Gaining this understanding is the goal of the other chapters in this book. Let's put up a giant "REMEMBER THIS" sign right here: The *reason* we're trying to understand one another is not only to draw closer, but so we can:

(1) build a financial cushion

(2) talk and come together about money

For the final few pages of this chapter, we're going to show you why those two elements are so important for thriving in love and money. (See the detailed results of the regression analysis and other data underlying these conclusions at shaunti.com/research.)[11]

Building cushion helps the relationship.

Over the years, much research[12] (including ours) has found that to have a healthy *relationship* (not just a

41

healthy bank account) it doesn't really matter how much income you have: What matters is living below that line. What matters is having some cushion, so you can pay your bills *and* have enough to go to the movies once in a while, or fix the dishwasher without building up credit card debt.

That cushion also acts as a buffer for your relationship. When the dishwasher breaks, you aren't as thrown; you aren't as likely to start blaming and bickering over whether your partner should have put that tip money in savings instead of spending it on new running shoes.

Having that discretionary income is closely correlated with avoiding dangerous tensions in the relationship—especially "withdrawing" tensions such as defensiveness, hiding purchases, doing money separately, or resignation. Meanwhile, having very little or no cushion is strongly correlated with a host of damaging marriage dynamics.

Building a cushion will almost certainly require some of the "technical" habits of managing money mentioned earlier. It is difficult to build cushion if you have a lot of debt, for example. It is also difficult to build cushion on a tight budget without, well, an actual budget.

But for most of us, unless we have cash coming out of our ears, it also requires something else that is often overlooked: the ability to talk about money and get on the same page with our partner.[13]

Being able to talk about money helps the relationship even more.

For many couples, talking about money ranks somewhere below cleaning the toilets or watching political debates with a cheerleader for the other party. In our Decision Analyst survey, our other main survey, 76 percent of respondents don't even want to budget because it is too hard (62 percent), because they will argue or not agree (51 percent), and/or a host of other unpleasant reasons.

This is a shame, because *all* our surveys found that being able to talk about finances is one of the most high-leverage things we can do to thrive in love and money. In the analysis of the young families survey, this is especially true if we can talk about money, as needed, without awkwardness—something that only comes with practice and empathy. Those who could do so were much, much more likely to avoid the most damaging, most aggressive tensions in their relationship.[14]

It is ironic that we may avoid talking about money in order to avoid tensions—*yet doing so creates far more of them!*

Here's the other startling finding: Being able to talk about money at all—even if it is awkward and uncomfortable—is more important than having financial cushion. In fact, we were startled to discover that when it comes to some of the most common worry-related money tensions—things like anxiety, stress, avoidance, and not feeling cared for—

if you have cushion, but cannot talk about it, it is likely to make your relationship *worse*.

Let me say that again. If you have more financial cushion in your life, but do not talk about money, you are more likely to have damaging tensions than if you had less money on hand, but could at least talk about it. In other words, our secret thought that more money would solve things ("We wouldn't fight if we just had more money") is completely wrong. As one financial planner agreed, "People think wealthier couples have it easier, because even if they aren't on the same page they surely won't fight when there's more than enough money to go around. But honestly, I think the opposite is true."

> It is ironic that we may avoid talking about money in order to avoid tensions—*yet doing so creates far more of them!*

Now, all this said, most people on the surveys said they absolutely *do* talk about money! For example, "We talk about money whenever we need to, without any difficulty" (57 percent on the Dynata survey), or "We *enjoy* discussions about budgeting" (56 percent on the Decision Analyst survey). Other surveys commonly find the same thing.

It would have been very easy for these people to give us a complex.

But then we looked deeper. We dug into the rest of the answers on the survey and realized that most of these folks aren't so much money communication Jedis as they are Pinocchios. For example, on the Decision Analyst survey, of those who said they like and don't avoid budgeting discussions, two-thirds *of those same people* also said elsewhere they felt a sense of dislike or futility around working on budgets! And on the Dynata survey, 60 percent of those claiming to talk without difficulty said elsewhere that they avoid talking about money because it gets awkward![15]

Chart 2.2: Every couple is different in how or whether they communicate about money. (Adjusted)[16]

We talk about money whenever we need to, without any difficulty.	**23%**
We talk about money whenever we need to, but it can be awkward, difficult, or stir up negative emotions.	**32%**
We probably avoid talking about it at times (don't talk about money as often as we need to), because it can be awkward, difficult, or stir up negative emotions.	**45%**
We don't talk about money as often as we need to, but for completely different reasons.	**1%**
TOTAL	**100%**

Source: Dynata survey.
Numbers presented exceed 100 percent due to rounding.

45

When we adjust the numbers to account for answers elsewhere on the survey, we see that *only 23 percent truly do appear to be able to talk about money without difficulty* (Chart 2.2).

But as you can see, the rest (77 percent) can't. They avoid it. Or they can talk if needed, but find it awkward and difficult.

The bottom line

When we look at all our research as a whole, we see that about 20 to 25 percent of us are really quite good at communicating and being connected around money. About 25 percent of us are really quite bad at it. And about 50 to 55 percent of us are in the massive middle, succeeding or failing depending on the situation (Chart 2.3). (See shaunti .com/research for a detailed breakdown of this bell curve.)

Chart 2.3 Connection and communication (or not) around money—the big picture

LES (MONEY) MISERABLES 25%	THE SO-SO MIDDLE 50-55%	THE BRIGHT SPOTS 20-25%

Why is the ability to talk about money so central? I (Jeff) was struck by something I heard on the popular podcast *The Tim Ferriss Show*. Mr. Ferriss mentioned having a friend who is a money manager to a lot of powerful people. This money manager told him, "I know [these clients] better than therapists they've been seeing for decades, within the first few hours, because money brings up everything. Talking about money brings up the full spectrum of someone's insecurities, fears, desires, neuroses."[17]

Talking about money simply brings up a lot we need to understand about each other. Which helps the relationship —no matter how much money you have.

"I see you"

In the movie *Avatar*, two alien cultures meet and often clash, as some try to understand one another. The main female character from the planet of Pandora tells an Earth soldier that their respectful greeting is "I see you." Later in the movie we learn that it doesn't just mean, "I see you standing here," it means, "I see *into* you, I understand you."

See into your spouse; the beautiful alien in your life.

See into yourself—which, when it comes to money, is just as important.

And use money as the window to do it. Don't just see your mate's reactions, feelings, fears, and perceptions—see your own too. This will help with everything in your marriage. And everything in your money as well.

The rest of this book is designed to help you do that: to give you a window into the deep places of our hearts and minds, to share what we found, and to show you what you might want to look for.

3 Can't Buy Me Love

Why my reasonable wants and your ridiculous wants often leave us wanting

Insight #1: We often do not value what our partner values.

When we first got married, we lived in Manhattan. I (Jeff) come from a blue-collar family and was very attuned to the fact that, with two recent graduate degrees from Harvard, we were starting out with extensive student loans. I worked long hours to hack away at our student loan debt, but we also wanted to enjoy the New York experience—especially the food! A couple of evenings a week, Shaunti and I would find a small, moderately priced restaurant and have dinner before I headed back to the office.

Unfortunately, Diet Cokes caused quite a few of those dinners to end on a low note.

It would start out great. We'd order reasonably priced food and I'd be happy. But then came the drink order. I'd ask for water and Shaunti would ask for a Diet Coke. I'd feel a slight twist in my stomach. Drinks in New York are expensive: $4.50 for something that costs the restaurant twenty cents.

I wouldn't share that with Shaunti, though, as I tried to enjoy our time together. But eventually the waiter would ask if we needed anything else. That's where the train would run off the rails.

I'd say no. But if she was still thirsty, Shaunti would order a second Diet Coke. And there's no such thing as free refills in New York.

In my mind, this was a ridiculous use of $9. I didn't realize it then, but subconsciously I began ascribing negative motivations to Shaunti—she's selfish, she doesn't appreciate how hard I'm working to reduce our debt (even though she was working plenty hard herself!), she's not careful with money, and so on. The evening would begin its downward slide.

It wasn't until several months of this that Shaunti realized she needed to explain what was happening in her mind—and I realized what was happening in mine.

I already knew that for some reason, Shaunti disliked the taste of water. She explained, "I just don't enjoy having a meal without a drink. If I can only have water, I'd rather not eat out. And I'm fine with not eating out and saving that money."

That one comment entirely changed my perspective. Why? I suddenly understood the *value* Shaunti put on having a drink with her meal. Before, I not only didn't value the same things she did—I thought what she valued was ridiculous. Yet if she had spent the same amount of money on something *I* placed value on, it would have been fine. My reaction would have been different if Shaunti had spent $9 on a dessert. (Because I would have gladly shared it!)

The painful part of this story is the long tail those assumptions can have. I *still* find myself ascribing negative motivations to Shaunti whenever I don't see the value in something she wants to buy.

The thing is, we all do this.

Different People, Different Values

I know it's a shocker, but you are married to someone who is different from you. They have vastly different things that matter to them. They hate spending $300 each month on supplies at Costco but readily drop $300 on dinners out. You don't care whether you eat in or out, as long as you pay via the cash-envelope method—which your spouse thinks is *way* too much trouble. You both want to give generously to your church, but sharply disagree over how much to give your kids or stepkids on their birthdays.

Each of you simply has different values. One of the most basic but crucial secrets to thriving in love and money is to look for and honor the reason your spouse feels the way they do.

Because here's the amusing part: Just as we all think we're above average drivers, we *all* think we know better about money. On the Dynata survey, nearly two-thirds of respondents felt this way (Chart 3.1).

You don't have to agree with your spouse. You don't even have to value what they do. In fact, there will be plenty of times you don't. But you will have a vastly better relationship once you make the effort to understand why something matters to them—even if it conflicts with what matters to you.

And sometimes the "something" that matters may not be a thing at all.

Chart 3.1: We are all above average.

I feel that I know more than my partner about managing money for our long-term happiness and well-being. **64%**

I feel that I am better than my partner at managing money to enjoy the present. **62%**

Source: Dynata survey.

Golf Robots, Giving, and Other Gaping Value Differences

In hundreds of interviews, we identified dozens of *types* of money-related factors that matter to each of us—physical items, experiences, processes for making money decisions, and so on. And any could be an opportunity for either frustration (if you don't recognize the value your partner places on something), or connection (if you do).

There's no way to include all the factors, but we have condensed them into six major categories. Ready to identify what applies to you? Let's tackle these one at a time.

What we value #1: Things, services, and experiences

This is the most obvious factor. We don't always value an *item*, *service*, or *experience* as much as our partner does. Usually because we don't understand the "why"—what it *means* to our spouse.

When asked to imagine a disagreement about what mattered in a fairly large purchase (for example, a basic refrigerator versus one with bells and whistles), nearly two-thirds of survey-takers on our Dynata survey (63 percent) said they at times have the subconscious feeling, "I just don't see the value in what my spouse sees as so important." This means that if our spouse feels we don't care about or value what matters to them (an opinion held by 51 percent of those on that survey), they're probably right!

Even more striking, 67 percent admitted they sometimes privately feel, "My partner isn't adequately thinking of all the important factors. If they would just look at it with an unbiased view, they would probably agree with me" (Chart 3.2).

Chart 3.2: In situations like the refrigerator scenario, do you ever feel, "My partner isn't adequately thinking of all the important factors. If they would just look at it with an unbiased view, they would probably agree with me"?	
Yes, I often/sometimes feel that way.	**67%**
No, I don't feel that way.	**33%**
TOTAL	**100%**

Source: Dynata survey. Shortened for presentation.

In other words: *This poor person isn't thinking clearly.* Of course our spouse feels our subconscious condescension, which starts things rolling downhill.

Early in our research, we conducted a focus group with five couples with young children. They all had a high money and relational IQ, having gone through a popular budgeting course and several marriage seminars. Yet as one couple described a particular conflict about money, the wife suddenly started crying.

The couple (we'll call them Josh and Carrie) have two young boys. Carrie misses the full-time job she left when they had their first child, but also loves being a mom and working part-time. Josh leads a large organization that employs hundreds of people in a public, high-stress government job, and is an avid golfer on Saturdays. Both clearly love and appreciate each other.

But when it came to understanding each other's motivations around money decisions, there were some gaps.

Their conflict started when Josh wanted to cancel their YMCA membership to save $100 a month; he said she could use the gym at the golf club where they were already members.

Carrie replied that yes, the Y was expensive, but it had features that were perfect for the kids, like an amazing pool with water slides. And her closest friends were members of the Y, not the golf club. She said now that the boys were starting preschool, she'd like to not give up on it.

Josh explained to the focus group, "But I told her there are so many cheaper options for working out, where you're not paying for the frivolous stuff, and I was just trying to lay those out there for her."

Unexpectedly, Carrie's eyes started to puddle. "I think because the Y doesn't benefit him, it feels like a frivolous extra expense. I lose ground in these disagreements, because I'm not contributing as much financially."

Josh shook his head. "Look, she could make $500,000 a year and we'd have the same conversation. It is about perceived value. That's just how I'm wired."

Suddenly, Carrie started crying. "*I* see value in it! The Y is close to where I drop the kids off, it allows me to take a quick break during the day, and I can meet up with my friends at the last minute. But for him, I guess a $1,200 golf robot has value!"

Wait, what? Everyone in the focus group was now thinking the same thing: *I'm so sorry you're crying, but what the heck is a golf robot?*

A bit on the defensive now, Josh shared that golf is his one leisure and exercise activity, but he hates lugging his clubs and a cart is $20. He'd rather walk. The solution is, in Carrie's words, a "golf robot." He said, "It will pay for itself in just over a year. It's a great value. Not to mention it makes me feel like I'm on Tour when it's traveling beside me over the course."

Suddenly, I (Jeff) had a mental image of C-3PO from *Star Wars* saying something like, "Master Josh, you are 163 yards from the pin, at the back of the green. A firm seven iron from here should do it!" I thought, *Josh, man, there is no way you are going to win this one.*

Over time we realized the real issue: Carrie and Josh had clear ideas of what was valuable to them, but just couldn't see and feel what their spouse did—even though they cared deeply about them. Like many of us, each had a tendency to think the other person was *wrong* in their judgments—and even disparaged what they valued.

For Josh, going to the gym is a transaction: You work out; you leave. He didn't see the Y as Carrie saw it: a close-by escape from chasing around small children, or a much-needed chance to see friends.

For Carrie, golfing is a transaction. And an already expensive one. Even calling the purchase a "golf robot" makes it sound absurd and extravagant. She didn't see that golf is Josh's one Zen moment in a stressful week, and this automated caddy (which is what it actually is) allows him to enjoy it much more—and will reduce his expenses in the long run. (Yes, we searched "golf robot" online, Some of you just did too.)

When we're in the middle of these disagreements, they appear to be just about the numbers. But hiding behind the discussion is something much deeper.

What we value #2: Enjoy today or save for tomorrow

Another type of value isn't a thing or an experience: It's a time frame. Do you place more value on enjoying today? Or on saving for tomorrow? We heard so many examples of this. As one woman explained,

> I work really hard, so I want to play a little. I try to save too, but I've never been as good at the "just don't spend money" thing. To me that is, "Don't have a life," but my husband says, "We can have a life—because we'll have money later." Yeah, but what if I die before? I want to spend it as I go! I do have discipline at work and with the kids, but not in this area. And money—it is freedom. Freedom to go out to eat. Or get a hotel on a weekend with my husband. Why are we working so hard if we can't enjoy some of the money?
>
> Both of us say, "Well, you're wrong." And we laugh because we can't both be right!

A similar disagreement is whether you should pay off debt before buying something, or whether debt is, up to a point, an acceptable avenue to get what you want or need (such as a particular experience while the kids or grandkids are "the right age").

This clash over today versus tomorrow can either resolve or become more acute once "tomorrow" arrives. Many people naturally evolve in how they view money in their later years—spenders may value saving more, and savers may value loosening up and enjoying life while they are in good health. Many others, however, feel their earlier values even more strongly.

Does every spending decision involve a trade-off?

One of the factors running under the surface is that there are two ways of viewing money when we are spending it. In our Dynata survey, 38 percent of people said money decisions always involve a trade-off: Spending something automatically means having less for something else. But 62 percent said that's not how they think of money at all, and are more likely to evaluate purchases on a case-by-case basis (Chart 3.3). (Because many people have asked about the gender stereotype on this, we should mention that, no, there was no correlation with gender.)

Not surprisingly, those who view every money decision as a trade-off are more likely to take the longer-term view, emphasizing saving. Those who view each decision as being about whether the item or experience is valuable on its own, assuming more money will come around, are more likely to choose to enjoy the moment.

Chart 3.3: As you go about day-to-day spending decisions, do you consciously think that most spending decisions involve a trade-off?	
Not really. I tend to evaluate whether we want or need something on a case-by-case basis.	**62%**
Yes. I have in mind that if I pay for one thing now, there will be less money for something else later.	**38%**
TOTAL	**100%**

Source: Dynata survey.

There are also cultural factors running underneath *many* of these different values—including this one. We personally see these in action in our own extended families, which, because of who our siblings married, are both culturally and racially diverse. (We are Caucasian, but our kids have just a few Caucasian cousins; the rest are a mix of Asian, Hispanic, and African-American.)

Here's just one example shared by a Southern California husband, whose view is certainly not universal but is something we heard many times.

In the Latino culture, family is everything. Families celebrate a child walking for the first time, birthdays, many things. We throw big family parties and meals and we'll spend a bunch of dollars we may not have. Someone might be struggling to make rent, but it's a birthday, so they'll drop $300 on Disneyland. We know we have to make rent, but we'll figure it out later. And probably do that as a family too.

What we value #3: The process of purchasing— how we make money decisions

People also value different *processes* for making money decisions. Here are a few examples:

Formal versus informal budgeting

We were surprised at the number of couples on the Dynata survey who diverged widely about whether they needed to implement an actual written budget (which only 19 percent had), or just a loose budget they kept in their heads (34 percent)—or no budget at all (39 percent). (Nine percent had developed an actual budget at some point, but were not using it.)[18]

This is the debate Jeff and I had been having for years. Since I tend to be the one who manages the logistics of paying the bills and balancing the accounts—both for our household and our business—I had a general idea of how much we spent each month, and how much we *could* spend, while still trying to save. I knew when we needed to cut back on other spending because our staff salaries would be higher than usual, or we had a major bill for the kids' activities.

Since we checked with each other before any major purchases, this informal approach was fine with me. I never wanted to take the time (or, to be candid, the emotional energy) to do an "official" budget.

It sounds crazy to "budgeteer" types, but I valued *not* having a budget. But that informal approach caused Jeff immense heartburn. One wife we interviewed captured Jeff's type of anxiety well:

> When I was single, I went through Dave Ramsey's Financial Peace University and set up a budget for myself. When we got married, I told Jack that I would love to set up a real budget. But he's more in the moment. He would say "It will work out, it will be okay." He knows it is a lot of *work* to get a real budget and that seems exhausting to him. But it's exhausting to me to *not* have a budget!! Like, exactly *how* is it going to work out?!

Flexibility versus structure

Whether or not a couple has an "official" budget, one person may value flexibility while the other wants more structure.

As one wife said, "I feel the compulsion to keep the budget to the letter, and he feels freedom to overlook it. And yes, I know the budget is a guideline and things come up. If your car blows up, then things change. But it's like any other good habit."

One father gave an example of how his adult daughter and her husband—who were very different—came to a compromise.

Kyle tends toward discipline: planning, budgeting, foregoing things, seeking out a good deal for vacation so they can go somewhere they didn't think they could afford. My daughter Shara is, "If I like it, I'm going to get it." It's not a sense of entitlement. She just looks at life that way.

When Kyle and Shara came together they found a middle ground. Each has a monthly amount they can use however they want. It gives her quite a bit of latitude. Until she runs out.

Last Saturday, I took her to Hobby Lobby to help her frame four pictures they've been waiting to put up in their new apartment. She's looking at everything and says, "Dad, I want your help, but I'm not sure all four will fit in my budget." I'm hearing these unnatural words come out of her mouth!

She calls Kyle and breaks the news. He surprises her by saying, "Let's get them all now and just cut back next month's budget."

She was so happy he was flexible *for* her. And he was really pleased she was honoring his desire to stick to a plan.

Kyle and Shara's solution was similar to ones we heard in multiple interviews with thriving couples. Couples who designate a pot of money that each spouse can spend however they like were much more likely to be happy in their marriage. More on that in the "what do we do about it" part of this chapter.

Now, let me (Jeff) make a key point: It is easy for a "planner-type" (like me) to label a more flexible spouse an "impulse buyer." We see what appear to be impulse buys as signs the spouse doesn't have a plan. Also, we tend to think that *not* buying on impulse means *we* have a plan. None of that is necessarily true!

When I go to the grocery store for a loaf of bread and a gallon of milk, that's what I walk out with. When Shaunti goes to the store for two things, she comes out with ten. So I assume she doesn't have a plan.

> Couples who designate a pot of money that each spouse can spend however they like are much more likely to be happy in their marriage.

But at some point I realized she does: Her plan is to not go back to the store multiple times. She knows we're almost out of sour cream or Hot Pockets (yes, our teenage son treats Hot Pockets like its own food group), so it's better to get them now.

Freedom versus accountability

A related set of values is the freedom to make financial decisions without having to check in—versus the desire to be consulted on spending decisions that affect both of you.

These values can clash badly.

As one woman told us, "I don't want to feel like I'm in a parent-child relationship where he's telling me what I can or can't do. I have had a full-time job since I was fifteen years old. I'm naturally an independent person. So if he says, 'I think we should stick with this plan' or 'We can't do this,' I feel like I'm in this box where he's telling me what I can't do. So I'm going to buck it."

That's not necessarily a healthy response to a spouse's (understandable) desire for some boundaries! But it's a feeling we heard multiple times.

A common solution we heard is to give general freedom under a certain purchase amount, while agreeing to consult each other for purchases over that amount.

One big expense versus a lot of little ones

This difference was captured well by this couple:

Him: I just don't make that many purchases. And when I do spend money, it is larger, like a flat-screen TV we saved for. She's much more likely to make lots of little purchases that add up over time. I see that as death by a thousand cuts.

Her: Uh, yeah! Because I'm the one going to the grocery store every day!

Him: (Laughing) Okay, okay. But still. She looks at it as individual purchases. I look at it as $15 multiplied by fifty trips—it's quite a lot.

Her: Do you want to eat or not?

On sale or full price?

Dozens of people in our interviews mentioned their annoyance that their partner didn't wait to buy something when it was on sale—or that they *only* bought something if it was on sale!

I (Jeff) definitely don't want to buy things unless they are a good deal—even if we need it and have the money for it. And then half the time I miss the deal or I wish I'd gotten it earlier.

Our daughter played volleyball through middle and high school, and we would watch many hours of games from uncomfortable bleachers. It didn't bother Shaunti, but it really bothered me. I kept looking up "stadium chairs" online, and they were always $35, which I thought was ridiculous. Shaunti kept bugging me to get one anyway, but I wouldn't. In our daughter's senior year, I walked into Costco and saw those same chairs for $15, plus a $4 rebate! I bought one for each of us, and we enjoyed using them—for the last half of the last season. Of course I wondered, *Why didn't I just get those chairs six years ago, to save my back??*

But I didn't tell Shaunti that.

The risk of the hard-and-fast restriction

In the research, we saw many spouses married to strict long-term saver types who initially gave up the flexibility they valued because they felt they "should" agree with their spouse and save nearly everything. Many of these men or women felt sheepish about asking for a more flexible budget.

But we also saw an ironic outcome. When only the value of the strict long-term saver is honored, it doesn't actually work well in the long term. (Just as it doesn't work well the other way around.) The spouse who valued current enjoyment sometimes became sad or resentful. And while there's certainly no excuse for breaking a financial agreement behind your spouse's back, we heard many examples of spouses who did just that after feeling like their partner was too restrictive and didn't care about what they valued.

Connor, a traveling salesman, and Kaya, a bookkeeper determined to be ready for retirement, were in their late twenties. In her view, if it didn't go toward the house or their retirement, they could do without. Eventually, Connor began to chafe about not having experiences he enjoyed, especially when he was working hard on the road. He said, "I started to think, 'I just got a bonus, and I deserve a break to go to this concert or this dinner, but I know she'll tell me no. So I'll put it on my credit card, and just pay it off each month.' But then I didn't always pay it off."

When he finally shared what had been going on, Kaya was stunned. "It was like finding out your spouse was unfaithful. But then I had to look at myself and ask, was some of this about me? I realized I didn't treat him as an equal partner in money management. He needed to be less selfish, but I needed to be more approachable and make decisions as a family. Changing our dynamic has been a relief. If you're not on the same page with *why* you're doing what you're doing, you'll never feel shared ownership."

What we value #4: Giving versus preserving

There are whole books written on the mindset of generosity and charitable giving. Which, in some cases, comes into conflict with the value of preserving and not "wasting" what one has.

First, just to lay this on the table, giving is a value for Jeff and me. For us, it is a faith thing that has transformed into a personal value thing. One husband's thoughts on this are similar to our own:

> I didn't necessarily start out as a giver, but sort of grew into it. I see in the Bible that God describes everything we have as belonging to Him and coming from Him. He says it is not good for us to hold too tightly to what we have, right? He says to trust Him in everything—and finances are probably the hardest thing to do that with.

That's why we tithe.* And He says He'll always take care of us. It's not a transaction—not "we give this so God does that" but a trust thing. But you can only build that trust by the scary steps of giving to Him and then watching Him honor His promise.

Not every couple will be unified in this value. Especially when it comes to "significant" giving.

An aeronautical engineer sitting beside me on a plane captured a common perspective: "My wife has got a great heart and she is more likely to say we need to give more at church. That was one of the big conflicts we had. Why are you donating so much to that? I mean, I give too. I don't mind, when it's something tangible. Like, we sponsor a child through World Vision. But just writing a big check to a church? There's got to be a balance."

A parallel value clash can occur when a couple values giving in different ways or for different purposes. Think about a contributing Democrat married to a contributing Republican these days, and you can see what we mean!

(We should note that while different values do impede alignment on giving, a greater issue—which often contributes to the values clash—is the simple inability of

---

* Note: A "tithe" means a "tenth." In the Bible, God says that since all we have comes from him, we should give back a tithe of what comes in, to be used for his purposes (such as help for the poor and support for religious workers serving others).

a husband and wife to sit down and talk about money. Helping couples overcome that hurdle has many ripple effects.)

What we value #5: Time versus money

One discussion nearly every couple has had is whether to value time over money, or money over time. Do you leave work early so you get to the crowded movie theater and stand in line to get tickets and good seats? Or do you buy the tickets online for the nicer theater with reserved seating, even though you'll pay a service fee?

Do you pay a house cleaner to come in once every few weeks to save you time and trouble? Or do you do it yourself?

Do you take the bus to and from work while your car is in the shop? Or do you take an Uber?

What we value #6: Doing it cheap and slow versus expensive and fast

Do we value the cheaper and/or do-it-yourself approach to something? (Fixing the plumbing, throwing the friend's birthday party, budget versus high-end hotels . . .) Or do we value convenience, atmosphere, experience, or speed, even if it means spending more money?

On projects, one of us may value the chance to try to do it ourselves the cheap way, first—hoping we never have to get to the expensive way. Sometimes that works and saves the family money—further confirming to that spouse that this is a valuable way of providing for the family. Alternatively, one spouse might feel the DIY approach causes so much angst or trouble, it just isn't worth it.

A couple in one focus group, Reed and Bobbie, described having to replace the vinyl liner in their old pool. Bobbie, who works in real estate, wanted to call a professional pool company to replace it. Reed, who doesn't work in real estate (foreshadowing), wanted to find someone on Craigslist.

Bobbie thought that was crazy, but Reed got annoyed that she wanted to call a higher-priced person right off the bat, so she let him handle it. Craigslist was consulted, Tyler quoted a great price, and work was agreed to. Unfortunately, it got off to a late start (picture Bobbie sitting beside Reed as he explains this to us, tightly holding her smile at bay). As Reed described it, "Tyler had the best intentions and tried to make progress, but he didn't have a car, so it made it tough to get to our house."

Bobbie is losing her self-control as a grin flickers across her face.

Finally, Reed surrendered and agreed to let Bobbie call the pool company.

What was going through their minds was *extremely* representative of what we'd heard from others.

Bobbie said, "Calling someone on Craigslist exposed you to safety issues, which was my number one concern.

Not to mention that I wanted the job done right and quickly—because I wanted to start using the pool! But I was willing to let Reed run with it. Even though I knew it was going to bug me the whole time."

As for Reed: "I honestly didn't consider the safety issue. I was focused on price. And frankly it was fun to see if I could make this work and save a ton of money for the family. When it works, it's like, 'I totally stuck it to the man and made this work for us.' This time, well . . . I got stuck. But it was definitely worth a try."

There are two highly competing values at work here. He wanted to provide by saving a lot of money, combined with a bit of achieve-something adventure ("Can I make this work?"). She wanted speed, safety, and I-won't-have-to-worry-about-it reliability. (In this case, those values happened to break down along fairly common gender lines, but that wasn't always the case in the research.) Neither of them even *thought* of the things the other person valued—much less thought to discuss them!

What are yours?

You as a couple can probably identify other factors, whether that is valuing risk for potential reward (entrepreneurs, unite!) versus valuing security, or valuing paying money to remove uncertainty (e.g., travel insurance) versus "Let's not worry about it until we have to."

What Do We Do about These Value Differences?

As you know from the last chapter, we are ultimately trying to understand how each partner feels around money so we can come together without tension, talk about it, and create a financial foundation we can both feel good about.

It turns out that trying to understand these value differences is a great starting point. Here are a few key tips that will help.

Tip #1: Next time you're at odds, assume there's a reason and ask, "Is this a value thing?"

Ask yourself: Is this something that matters to my spouse that I am just not seeing—or not valuing? Or maybe even, is there something here that matters to *me* that's being triggered, that I might not be aware of? And more to the point: How can I understand my spouse without judging them—even if I don't agree?

As one couple described a recent, fairly sharp conflict, the husband suddenly began to realize what had been behind a particular reaction. His wife said, "I wish I'd known. I think knowing the 'why' would help couples."

He nodded. "I guess we have to always think, 'There is a reason,' so we can search within ourselves and figure out the why."

Tip #2: Figure out your motivations—and address those.

Remember the pool-liner story, where the real estate agent let her husband have his attempt at Craigslist do-it-yourself? Imagine that instead of one person letting the other have full say for a while (in which case one "wins" and the other "loses"), the couple had tried to figure out what each cared about most, and had tried to address those underlying things. It might have come out like this:

What I care about / What is motivating me

Reed:

- I want to save money.
- It is fun to see if I can make it work.
- It's stupid to pay so much money for a pool liner, so on principle I want to make it cost less.

Bobbie:

- I want to be able to use the pool by next Friday.
- I don't like having someone around the house who we don't know, who wasn't vetted by a company.
- I've seen this process many times on the job, and generalists on Craigslist usually don't have the tools or technical skills for something this specialized.

If they had done this, they could have arranged things so that most of what mattered to both of them would be covered. Reed could have agreed to work at home the days the handyman was working. Or the handyman could have been hired with the caveat that his fees would be paid only *if* he hit the tight schedule marks he said he would—and if not, Bobbie would immediately hire the pool company. And she would agree to treat Reed like a superhero if his plan worked—and not rag him if it didn't!

We do not need to be perfect at talking things through in order to address this stuff well; we just need to start figuring out what we each care about.

Tip #3: Consider setting aside an agreed-upon monthly amount that each of you can spend however you wish.

Since ultimately much of this frustration comes because one spouse doesn't think the other spouse's item or experience is "worth it," it makes a huge difference when each partner has a monthly amount of money set aside to spend however they like without having to check in with the other person. On two different surveys, those who said they "definitely" did this were *much more likely to be at the highest level of happiness in marriage than those who said they did not.*[19]

This is important, so it bears repeating: Couples were far more likely to be at the highest level of marital happiness if each spouse had a monthly amount they could spend any way they wanted—whether that was framing pictures for the new apartment, or a concert during a business trip. Unfortunately, only 21 percent of couples "definitely" did this (26 percent said they tried, and 53 percent said they didn't), but we can make a really good case that all of us should look into doing this!

Tip #4: Recognize that logic could lead the two of you to two different conclusions.

Honest discussion reveals something we need to recognize: What is underneath our values is usually more a matter of the heart than the head. Even if we like to fool ourselves into believing otherwise.

Most of us think, "The way I've organized our finances is the most logical." It just makes sense that we prioritize family adventures while the kids are small. Or, it just makes sense that we should be saving money and prioritizing our future! But in the end, what "just makes sense" to us is often not an intellectual construct, but a feeling.

I (Jeff) was listening to *The Arthur Brooks Show* podcast when I was startled by a statement of his guest, author Dr. Curt Thompson, a psychiatrist with a specialty in neurobiology.[20]

Dr. Thompson said, "I'm not convinced that anybody ever chooses to not follow [a particular path] just because of intellect, because I think when we start talking about intellect, we're talking about a phenomenon that . . . doesn't exist in the brain apart from emotion."

He described how various friends claimed certain decisions were based on an "intellectual enterprise" but his neurobiological expertise "makes it really hard for me to be persuaded of that." Mostly because, he said, the brain doesn't work that way. The structure and processing of the brain means that human intellect cannot exist without emotion.

As a result, he concluded, "Human beings never make decisions because they make sense. We make sense of things that feel right."

We don't realize it, but we take what matters to us and wrap our justifications around it. At the same time, we layer on very important relationship expectations about what matters.

Which leads to our final action step.

Tip #5: Be willing to reexamine what we value.

Sometimes something has become a jealously guarded value—and we should probably examine whether it should be. Personally, we think this is particularly important for those who hold to the Judeo-Christian belief that "our" money isn't really ours, but God's. One financial ministry director at a large church put it well.

Ultimately, we have to take a close look at what we value. For example, the feeling that I deserve to have a Starbucks every morning. For years, I didn't think about the fact that I was using $5 of God's money each time. It's scary, but we need to be willing to ask God how He wants His money used. It's not just "Oh, you can tithe and then do whatever you want with the other 90 percent." That's not real stewardship.

When people go through the financial class at our church, so many end up saying, "This was not about money; this was about the heart." If you don't fix the heart it doesn't matter if you're more effective with money: You'll still be greedy, you'll just be better at it! My objective has always been to help people get their heart free.

"I Want You to Value Me"

Money is a matter of the heart. Of what we care about. Throughout the day, subconsciously, each of us is asking our spouse, "Do you care about me?" "Do you value what matters most to me?"

I (Jeff) am silently asking Shaunti: Do you value that what matters to me is to avoid the tension of living paycheck to paycheck, and to have money set aside for the future?

Shaunti is silently asking me: Do you value that what matters to me is flexibility to *not* live with the stringent spending constraints you are perfectly happy with?

And when it comes to money, the only way to show that we do value our spouse is to take on faith that what our partner *tells* us matters to them *really does*. Again, this doesn't mean you always agree. Sometimes empathy and understanding our partner's values won't solve everything. One or both of us might value something we truly cannot afford! If either of you sees warning signals, the other needs to care enough to listen. But the more practice *we* have listening, caring, and understanding, the more likely it is that our spouse will listen when those warning signs arise.

And as each of us honors the values that matter to our spouse, we are far better positioned to come together on values that go far beyond money.

4 Things That Go Bump in the Night

How we use money to fight our fears and worries—
and end up spooking our partner instead

Insight #2: We each have fears our partner doesn't comprehend and use money to try to relieve them—which often makes our partner's fears worse.

Becky and Tim had been married for thirty years. For much of that time there was strife around how many hours he worked and how little time they had together.

Tim's hours were long and stressful, and he had to miss a lot of family experiences. This really bothered him and Becky, but the bonuses were great. She enjoyed inviting friends and ministry partners from church to their beautiful home. They took nice vacations and paid for all three of their daughters to be on traveling club volleyball teams during high school—although Becky was often the only one to see the games.

Becky continually asked Tim to cut back. To worry less about the next deal and more about being present with the family. Tim said he would love to, but someone had to pay for the mortgage and the volleyball fees and the new curtains she just got for their bedroom. Someone had to save for college and retirement. And pay the large credit card bill from the beach trip.

Becky replied that her salary covered a lot of those extras, and she was totally willing to *not* go to the beach if that would let him slow down . . . especially since connecting and slowing down was the whole point of the beach trip!!

Over the years they made little progress. He felt exhausted and she felt lonely—especially once the girls were out of the house. They grew apart.

When he wanted them to move so he could take a lucrative promotion across the country, it brought their issues to a head. Painfully, they started discussing divorce. Becky asked Tim, "If we get divorced, when would you take that position and move?"

Tim shook his head. He wouldn't take the position at all. If they got divorced, he would quit his firm entirely and find another job. One with fewer hours and less stress.

Becky was floored. What she had been pleading unsuccessfully with him to do for more than two decades, he would suddenly be willing to do if they were divorced.

It all comes down to one thing—or maybe two.

Tim and Becky's situation is an unusual version of a very common story; we've heard it in thousands of forms over the years. The details and outcomes may be different, but under the surface is the same universal factor: fear.

Actually, there are two distinctly different *sets* of fears in play. And because we tend to have opposite fears, we often don't recognize that the other person's fear is there—much less that a huge amount of tension over money (and everything else) is impacted by it.

Since we began doing social research in 2003, one of the most consistent and important trends we've seen is that there are *internal* differences between men and women (including neurobiological differences) that lead to *external* patterns and misunderstandings in male-female relationships.[21]

Some of this will sound stereotypical, but keep in mind that we're digging into why these stereotypes exist in the first place. Also, these dynamics are common but by no means universal. You and/or your spouse might not relate to some of these factors—or relate more to what is common to the opposite gender. The key is to be aware of what *is* applicable to you and your partner. Especially since what is applicable is often hidden.

One note: There are actually three extremely foundational aspects underneath *why* we and our spouse feel the way we do—our different fears, different reasons for them,

81

and different ways of handling them. Thus this chapter is a bit longer, as it is essentially three mini-chapters in one.

The Impact of Fear

Imagine for a moment that you have a fear of heights and are standing on the edge of a cliff with absolutely nothing between you and a 1,000-foot free fall into the canyon below. What are you *actually* afraid of? You're afraid of plummeting to your death, of course! So you are very attuned to how close you are to the lip of the canyon, right? You're literally on edge about it. Standing close to the lip, it's difficult to think about anything else. So what do you do?

You back away. Perhaps you build a railing. If you are particularly afraid of heights, you might decide to build a twenty-foot wall—even if it blocks your view.

And you may get very, very irritated with your partner if they beckon you forward to take a picture. "It'll be fine!" they say. "C'mon, what are you worried about?"

Two different "cliffs," two different fears, two different ways of handling those fears

Men and women tend to deal with two different sets of primary fears. Unlike a fear of heights, these two fears aren't always conscious or easily explained—to ourselves, much less our partner. Regardless, we're subconsciously "on edge" about them. We shy away from getting too close to disaster. We are eager to take action to protect ourselves—and find it completely confounding that our partner might not think action is necessary!

To make things even more interesting, not only do we tend to have two different sets of fears, we tend to *handle* them differently.

For the rest of this chapter, we will take turns describing how the opposite sex thinks. Whenever you see a section about men, it will be from Shaunti, talking to the women. Whenever you see a section about women, it will be Jeff, talking to the guys.

Let's start with how this works for men, and then switch.

from **SHAUNTI**

Men fear they won't be able to provide.

Ladies, men tend to have this concern: Am I going to be able to provide for my family? Are we going to have enough? Even if things are fine financially, most men are on edge about financial provision—both for today and for the future. Lurking constantly beneath the surface is the feeling: "Our finances are okay . . . until they aren't."

Most men have deep self-doubt about whether they are up to the task (more on that in a moment), so they never feel like they can let down their guard. If they do, things could fall apart.

As one man put it, "What drives me is fear of failure. My wife may see us as being sound financially, but I see us having so far to go. And what we do have could begin to slide away. I always have to be thinking about it."

from SHAUNTI ● **For men, "security" means financial security— it keeps the family away from the edge.**

In multiple previous studies, we have seen a deep desire—even a compulsion—among most men to provide for and protect their wives and children. In every study, at least seven out of ten men are either always thinking about this or subconsciously dealing with it (Chart 4.1). At its core, that compulsion appears to be driven by fear more than logic, and appears to be ever-present if the man has a spouse and children. (In fact, through this study and our previous ones, we've seen that the desire to provide is

Chart 4.1. (MEN): Under what circumstances do you think about your responsibility to provide for your family?	
Never	3%
Only when I'm unemployed or facing financial challenges	6%
It's occasionally in the back of my mind	20%
It's often in the back of my mind	21%
It's something I'm conscious of most of the time	50%
TOTAL	**100%**

Source: Survey of men from *For Women Only*

even there among single men and those who are married without children; it's just more quiet. Once a man has his first child, the desire appears to grow into a compulsion.)

In your man's heart, there is a real risk of the family "falling" financially! So he *needs* to build financial security as a barrier against that possibility. This doesn't mean he's the one physically paying the bills and being in charge of money for the household (in our surveys, women were slightly more likely to manage the finances than men). But he *is* focused on his ability to provide.

One husband explained, "I look for every opportunity to provide, and that's probably why I look for every reason *not* to spend money. For me there is a fear of not having, so there is always more to put away. Whereas my wife says, 'God is going to provide regardless, and this is an opportunity to do something the family would enjoy.'"

Another husband, in an uncertain season in his job, said, "I'm always looking for a way to be free from worry. But if I'm honest, it's impossible. I thought I would feel *so* much better if I had three months' worth of expenses in savings, but I still worried. With six months' worth, the same thing. The goalposts move."

But a man's drive to provide is not just a bulwark against fear. Building that bulwark is, to him, a primary way he can show you and the family how much he cares.

I have heard so many men say something like this programmer did:

> I love my wife. But I can't seem to get it across in a way she'll believe. I guess I'm not good enough with words. But I can *show* her I mean it. I've been putting in a lot of hours for about two years on this big systems integration project, and it's exhausting but the overtime is really lucrative. I hate being gone, but it's one of the main ways I can say "I love you."

This desire to provide is such a part of who men are that the vast majority said they would feel this way even if their wives made enough to provide for the family on their own (77 percent, according to the Decision Analyst survey). This is radically different from how we women tend to feel in the reverse situation (at least once kids are in the equation). On our first nationally representative survey (SSI), only 42 percent of mothers felt a compulsion to provide if their spouse earned all or most of the income.[22]

Just as surprising: Men who describe themselves as spenders are almost as likely to feel this compulsion as men who describe themselves as savers, especially once kids come along. On our SSI survey both "spender" and "saver" men were much more likely to always be consciously thinking about the need to provide than even saving-oriented women (Chart 4.2).

Which is probably why many men are completely befuddled that their spouse doesn't see the overwhelming primacy of this need like they do.

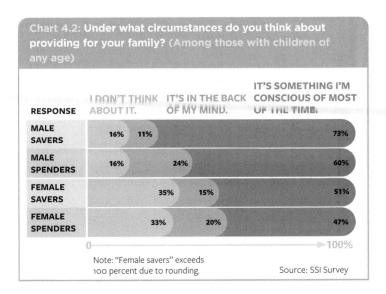

Chart 4.2: Under what circumstances do you think about providing for your family? (Among those with children of any age)

RESPONSE	I DON'T THINK ABOUT IT.	IT'S IN THE BACK OF MY MIND.	IT'S SOMETHING I'M CONSCIOUS OF MOST OF THE TIME.
MALE SAVERS	16%	11%	73%
MALE SPENDERS	16%	24%	60%
FEMALE SAVERS	35%	15%	51%
FEMALE SPENDERS	33%	20%	47%

0   100%

Note: "Female savers" exceeds 100 percent due to rounding.

Source: SSI Survey

Women (both savers and spenders) were *twice* as likely as men to not think or worry about providing very much; about one-third assume it will all just work out.

With all that in play, you can see how this one truth *alone* might account for a lot of frustration and heartache between spouses!

from SHAUNTI

This fear is fueled by his greatest vulnerability.

Why is your strong, competent, confident husband so affected by this particular fear? Because if he's like most men (76 percent) he doesn't feel nearly as strong, competent, or confident as he looks (Chart 4.3). I (Shaunti) can

Chart 4.3 (MEN): Do you ever feel, "I'm not always as confident as I look?"	
I feel like this regularly/sometimes.	**76%**
I rarely or never feel like this.	**24%**
TOTAL	**100%**
	Source: Survey of men for *The Male Factor*

still remember my shock years ago when I began researching how men privately think. I learned just how much they doubt themselves every day.

As one charismatic, self-assured man recently put it: "Us guys are insecurity walking around, but we don't want people to know it."

The thing is, their insecurities are different from ours. You know that "Am I lovable?" question we women have, deep down? Well, guys don't have that question! Instead, most guys are subconsciously asking the questions, "Am I able? Do I have what it takes?"*

You may think this sounds ludicrous, but it means your husband *truly* fears he won't be enough to keep your family from pitching over the edge financially and falling to the rocks below.

---

* These are foundational concepts. See *For Women Only* and *For Men Only* for how these vulnerabilities play out every day, in ways that go far beyond money. To be clear: To some degree we're all insecure about everything. But these are the insecurities most likely to be a particularly raw nerve for men or for women.

Even though difficulties in providing are often external (the economy, a difficult client, a truck that breaks down at the wrong time) even the most talented man might feel he's just a few mistakes from getting fired. Or from his business going south.

Several years ago, when I spoke at a retreat for a small group of successful business owners, several provided candid interviews. One wife told me:

> You asked if Travis still felt a compulsion to provide? I had to laugh about that one. He worked so hard for twenty-five years, and it was often stressful. So when he finally sold the company, I was grateful we had so much cash we would never have to work again. The downtime lasted two months, and then he started looking for companies to buy. I was like, "Honey, what are you doing?" He got a bit angry and said, "What? You think this will last the rest of our lives?!" I was like, "What are you talking about? Of COURSE it will!"

from JEFF  **Women are more likely to be on edge about closeness.**

Okay, let's switch sides. Guys, women think about money too. In fact, women are just as likely to be "savers" as men. But for our wives, family finances are less likely to create the gut-level "cliff fear" they do for us.[23] Instead, a woman's cliff fears tend to be *non*-financial: Is everyone okay? Are *we* okay? Does he *really* love me? Are we always going to be close? Are the kids feeling loved?

Even in a great relationship, these concerns are running under the surface and are triggered more easily than most men realize. This edginess in our wives is more subconscious than ours, but is nevertheless very real: "Our marriage and children are healthy . . . until they aren't" (Chart 4.4).

As one woman put it, "Yes, of course I think about money too, but I value *us*; and I'm more afraid of losing *us* than I'm afraid of losing money."

And yes, it might sound crazy that a relationship cliff could seem scarier than a financial one—but it's because our wife (if she is like most women) has a completely different insecurity than we do. (More on that shortly.)

Chart 4.4 (WOMEN): Under what circumstances do you think about your relationship, whether it is going well or how your husband/significant other feels about you?	
Never	12%
Only when we are in a really difficult season of our relationship	20%
It's often/occasionally in the back of my mind	50%
It's something I'm conscious of most of the time	19%
TOTAL	100%

Source: Survey of women from For Men Only
Numbers presented exceed 100 percent due to rounding.

For example, suppose she's worried because you were angry with her when you drove away to work, or because your sensitive middle-school daughter is going off to yet another day of dealing with mean girls at school. Once that concern is triggered, the cliff looms large in her eyes: *Is it going to be okay?* There are so many ways to fall over that cliff—and her mind imagines them all.

from JEFF For women, their top "security" is emotional security; that's what keeps the family away from the edge.

Thus your wife is very motivated to ensure you two don't come anywhere close to that edge. And the main way she does that is by working to be sure you and she (and the family) have time together. Time to talk and build connection. Time to do fun things together, share meaningful experiences with the kids, and ensure your kids know Mom and Dad are there for them.

In fact, guys, this need for emotional security and closeness is probably so primal for your wife that if she had to, she would give up financial security to get it; 70 percent of married women told us just that (Chart 4.5). (Again, note the important exceptions: 30 percent didn't.)

And this isn't just a vague desire. Most women are willing to make practical trade-offs to stay far away from the edge of that cliff. On the Decision Analyst survey, 62 percent of women said they would rather have their husbands

91

Chart 4.5 (MARRIED WOMEN): If you had to choose between two bad choices, would you rather endure . . .	
Financial struggles	**70%**
Struggles arising from insecurity or lack of closeness in your relationship	**30%**
TOTAL	**100%**
	Source: Survey of women from *For Men Only*

take a much-lower-paying job that would allow for closeness instead of distance, and would willingly make the lifestyle adjustments to do so. If we include those who are neutral (in other words, those who would support a husband if *he* wanted to take that job), fully 76 percent of women would trade their lifestyle and financial security to get more of *him*.

from JEFF

 **Her fear is fueled by her greatest vulnerability.**

Most women have underlying questions about whether they are lovable, beautiful, and valuable, and they don't go away just because you said, "I do." (Any more than your self-doubt goes away just because you're successful at your job.) In marriage, it simply morphs into "Does he *really* love me? Is he glad he married me?" On our *For Men Only* survey, this was the case for 82 percent of women.

You may be questioning whether you have the ability to provide for her and the kids; she may be questioning whether she is enough for *you*.

We both care—we're just watching different cliffs.

As you can tell, the cliff a husband is seeing is usually very different from the cliff a wife is seeing.

All that said, it is extremely important to note that having different primal fears and needs doesn't mean women don't care about finances and men don't care about relationships. When it comes down to a head-to-head contest between the two, both men and women on our surveys say that of course relationships are more important in the end.

The issue is that, unlike women, most men simply don't believe there could *be* a slide in the relationship! So for them, *of course* we need to put all our energy into ensuring our finances are secure—even if it means sacrificing time together.

> You may be questioning whether you have the ability to provide for her and the kids; she may be questioning whether she is enough for *you*.

So much of our conflict and heartache in marriage comes because we simply don't realize the other person is trying to stay away from a different edge.

Think back to the story of Tim and Becky at the beginning of the chapter.

She asked, "Why would you leave your job *now* if we're getting divorced?"

His answer: "I only do this job for you guys."

Windows, windows, everywhere

Not only are our fears and worries different, but the *way* we handle them is different too. Which causes additional disconnects! We cover these differences in *For Women Only* and *For Men Only*, but here are the basics.

Think of your mind like a computer desktop. The thoughts and feelings you're dealing with (or worrying about!) are the open windows or screens.

Perhaps because of the structure of the male brain, men tend to have one window open at a time. They think about something (*Huh . . . why did the Lions trade for that guy?*), process it, click the X button, close that thought window, and open up the next one. (*This marketing plan won't work.*) It's sequential.

Also, (very important) men can generally close windows that are bothering them. Worried about his sister's flight delay messing up the surprise party *and* worried about the marketing plan? No problem! Click the X button on the party! Done!

Women's minds, by contrast, have ten windows open at once. Or twenty. And they bounce back and forth between all of them at the same time. There are thoughts (*That spreadsheet has an error somewhere*), feelings (*I'm sad Lucy is getting picked on at school*), questions (*If Suzanne's flight is delayed, what does that mean for the party?*), worries (*Should we have kept Nate home from school? I hope he's okay. Do we need to take him to the doctor?*), and more. (Yes, guys, I know what you're thinking. It is indeed exhausting! If you want an eye-opening experiment, turn to your wife and ask, "What is on your mind *right now*?")

Just as important, a woman usually *cannot* easily click the X button and close windows that are bothering her. Those worries keep popping up until she takes action to address them. And the closer a worry comes to being one of her "cliff fears" about whether your relationship or the kids are okay, the more she'll feel the need to do so.

from JEFF For her, the wallet might *be* the X button that closes her window.

As it turns out, "taking action" includes spending money. According to our interviews and focus groups, three out of four women are willing to spend money if that's what it takes to close an open worry-window that is concerning them (Chart 4.6).

For example, does a child seem sick and miserable? Moms seem to be much more willing to pay to take the child to the doctor "just in case"—even though dads love

Chart 4.6 (WOMEN): Are you willing to spend money to close an emotional "window" that is bothering you?	
Yes	**75%**
No	**25%**
TOTAL	**100%**

Source: Compilation of event polls, interviews and focus groups 2017–2019.[24]

their kids just as much. Why? Because it would help close their worry window. Dads were far more likely to think (or say), "Just keep him home from school for a day or two and he'll get over it. It isn't something to worry about yet." (A woman has no idea what he even *means* by "don't worry about it yet"!)

from SHAUNTI

 For him, the wallet is the only thing that doesn't have an X button and can't be closed!

Ironically, despite so many men being puzzled by why a woman would "allow" something to bother her, there is one subject that a man handles exactly the same! In most cases, his ability to provide is a worry window he can't easily close. And it becomes excruciating if a legitimate "Am I going to be able to provide?" window is open (rather than just the usual cliff fear always lurking in the back of his mind).

Say the boss comes by his cubicle on Friday afternoon and says, "Bill, we just learned our revenue will be way down this year. I need to see you in my office Monday morning." Suddenly Bill knows *exactly* what it feels like to not be able to close a bothersome open window! Actually, "bothersome" is not the right word. It is agonizing. It's there 24/7 and will continue to be there until he is reassured or until he takes action steps to stop the looming fall over the financial cliff.

This is also why a man who hasn't been able to prevent a fall over the cliff—who has been laid off, can't get a good job, or feels he actually *isn't* providing well—can so easily fall into depression and apathy. It is far too painful to have the "you've failed" window open and screaming at him all the time, especially if he's tried and failed (in his mind) over and over again. For some men, instead of yet again confirming that he is not enough, it is far less painful to just check out.

How we use money to feel better about ourselves

Now that we've looked at our fears and worries in more detail, let's look at the surprising, subconscious ways we use money to assuage them.

We use money as an antidote to our insecurities.

We sometimes use money to feel better about ourselves.

Before I go any further, from a faith-based perspective, you may be thinking, "But we should get our security from the Lord, not from money!" Yes, we should. We all have holes in our heart that only God can fill. But in our imperfect state, all of us tend to look to many other things to fill those holes. We aren't endorsing this dynamic, but we need to understand it. It explains *a lot* about what is going on in our spouses and ourselves when it comes to money.

Nearly two-thirds of men and women say they use money to feel better about themselves, even if they've never thought about it that way before (Decision Analyst survey). And because we often don't know our spouse even *has* certain insecurities, we *definitely* don't understand why they would use money to feel better about them.

Let's look briefly at some of the trends we saw. (As before, Shaunti will explain the guys' side, while Jeff will explain the women's.)

from
SHAUNTI

A man's antidote

Ladies, a man is looking for an antidote to feeling like an imposter—whether at work, home, or any other place. And as you can see (Chart 4.7), when asked to choose ONE factor that would make him feel better about himself, by far the top answer (45 percent) was to be seen as someone who was respected or did things well. Another 22 percent of men said knowing they had a lot of money in the bank would be their top path to feeling better about themselves. As one man put it, "For men, finances are a scorecard. A direct measure of their

Chart 4.7: Many people have insecurities or ways they wish they were different. Imagine you could have one physical or emotional factor that would make you feel better about yourself. What ONE factor would you choose?		
	MEN	**WOMEN**
To be seen as someone who gets things done well / To be seen as someone who is respected	**45%**	**24%**
To feel special and "worth something" / To feel and be seen as attractive (beautiful, handsome, physically appealing)	**16%**	**41%**
All other factors combined	**39%**	**35%**
TOTAL		**100%**

Source: Decision Analyst Survey.
Note: excludes those who said they have no insecurities.

self-worth. It is an outward sign that shows he is good at what he does. It is a visible result of diligence and discipline."

In total, then, 67 percent of male respondents chose something related to achievement or respect as their top factor. This businessman summarized it well.

Getting things done, providing—that is the emotional measuring stick of a man. I think women miss how insecure and vulnerable we are. You may not realize how much you can calm the monster when you see that vulnerability and are tender with it, instead of challenging it. We're so hoping to hear, "You're doing a great job."

It all starts with providing an income. But it goes far deeper than just being a breadwinner. It means providing protection. It means being the best husband on planet earth. Being a great father. And when we feel we have failed in any capacity, it cuts us to our core.

Think of it this way: If a man is using money to feel better, it is probably to reassure himself that he *is* good at what he does, that he *is* worthy of respect. Here are a few common patterns we heard:

> "Getting things done, providing—that is the emotional measuring stick of a man. I think women miss how insecure and vulnerable we are. . . . We're so hoping to hear, 'You're doing a great job.'"

Saving money. Building up a large bank balance or investment account might be your man's way of saying, "I'm doing a good job." (Of course, if he doesn't like the balance, he would feel the opposite.) As one man told us, "I just want to make my wife happy. But I can't measure that. But am I providing well for her? Money in the bank—that's something I can measure."

Treating the people he loves. Another way a man might try to "succeed" is by making sure you and the kids have what you want. If you're married to a guy who is more of a spender than a saver, you might have read the earlier part of this chapter and wondered why he spends money if he is supposedly so worried about financial security! But for him, being able to buy you something nice or provide cool experiences or fund the family vacation is a way of saying he is doing okay as a husband or father.

Some of our closest friends, who I'll call Danielle and Kyle, gave us a great example of this. Both are conservative with money, and Danielle's new favorite place was the local Goodwill store. She was proud that she could find surprisingly cute stuff there for $5. Wanting to share her new Goodwill hobby with her husband, she took him with her one Saturday afternoon. Later, they told us what happened:

> *Danielle:* You know how Kyle is so laid-back, right? Well, as we walked around the store, he started getting agitated. He said, "I hate it here!" and he actually had to leave and wait for me in the parking lot.
>
> *Kyle:* I had no idea why I was upset. I've always hated people who put on airs, so I have no problem with wearing secondhand clothes. But I was so disturbed. As I processed it later, I realized what I was feeling: You're my wife, you deserve better than this. I want

101

to take care of you. I can give you enough money to go buy a new shirt!

Buying trophies. Remember the golf robot in chapter 3? Remember Josh's sidebar comment about why he wanted it? "It makes me feel like I'm on Tour when it's traveling beside me over the course." That may not have been such a minor reason after all. Just as with many grown-up toys, it made him feel cool, notable, like he was a higher class of player. Since men want *others* to see them as worthy of respect, some will spend money on things for others to admire.

Handling money well. Not everyone can make a lot of money. But as one man said, "How you handle what you have is worthy of respect. If you take what you've got and use it well for your family, it is so much more appealing than someone who inherited a lot of money. It's like when you see a great athlete who became great through sheer effort. As opposed to the guy with all the tools to be a great athlete who doesn't practice."

Having a wife who handles money well. One man said, "It sounds bad, but inside we want other guys to look at us and go 'wow.' And that includes about our wives. Not just that they're beautiful or smart or accomplished, but that they handle money well. It hurts a lot if my financial house is out of order because my wife makes certain decisions. It makes it harder for me to get respect from others."

Doing it himself to save money. We heard this many, many times. One way a guy feels better about himself is if he can do the DIY version of a project—fixing the plumbing, tinkering with the car, MacGyvering the broken closet shelves. This is both another way of providing and also a way of feeling like he conquered something. Especially if he gets kudos for it.

from **JEFF**

A woman's antidote

Guys, a woman tends to look for antidotes to her underground suspicion that she's really not special and that her husband will wake up one day and say, "Why am I married to *her*?!" Referring back to Chart 4.7, you can see that when respondents were asked to choose ONE factor to make them feel better about themselves, by far the top answer among women (41 percent) was to feel special, attractive, and worth something. As one woman poignantly described it,

> For me, I have come to see that when I want to wear nice clothes, or when I feel bad when I look at my friends' vacations on social media, it is about self-esteem. Deep down there's a feeling we don't deserve to be accepted, right? Why would my husband love *me*? He's amazing! It doesn't make *sense* for him to love me.

Just as with us as men, the actual *way* our wives seek reassurance about themselves could mean spending or saving. That said, it was very clear that one of the most common patterns we heard was "retail therapy"—even among women who are definitely more savers than spenders! So let's tackle that "antidote" first.

"Retail therapy." Yes, it's a stereotype. But many of us have seen this dynamic and been puzzled by it. On average, guys are more likely to be search-and-destroy shoppers: move in, quick kill, move out. So what is the appeal for our wives of wandering around a giant pedestrian mall? Why does my wife enjoy going to Target, the consignment store, or Costco?

She's not alone. In our Dynata survey, 54 percent of women agreed, "When I have had a hard week, sometimes it just makes me feel better about myself to go shopping for something new—even if it is at a consignment store or I don't buy much." Only 33 percent of men thought that made any sense at all. (See Chart 4.8.)

Surprisingly, "retail therapy" is also quite prevalent among women who are generally oriented toward saving. In fact, even saving-oriented women are more likely to use shopping as an antidote than spending-oriented men! And as you can imagine, if you are a saver married to a spender, there is probably a huge gap in understanding the desire for retail therapy. (Of course, I—*ahem*—have no idea what that feels like.)

Exactly why does "retail therapy" make so many of our wives feel better? When Shaunti spoke at a convention for 6,000 churchgoer moms, she mentioned this research project from the stage. Roughly 75 percent of those in

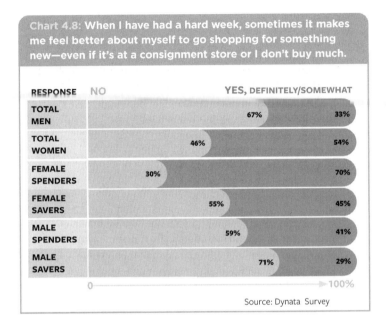

Chart 4.8: When I have had a hard week, sometimes it makes me feel better about myself to go shopping for something new—even if it's at a consignment store or I don't buy much.

RESPONSE	NO	YES, DEFINITELY/SOMEWHAT
TOTAL MEN	67%	33%
TOTAL WOMEN	46%	54%
FEMALE SPENDERS	30%	70%
FEMALE SAVERS	55%	45%
MALE SPENDERS	59%	41%
MALE SAVERS	71%	29%

0 ▶ 100%

Source: Dynata Survey

attendance raised their hands when she asked how many would go shopping to feel better about themselves. She invited anyone who had an insight on *why* to come visit her at the booth of Thrivent, our research sponsor. The booth was besieged for the rest of the day!

Here are a few common reasons that came out of that input and the rest of our research.

It makes her feel new. For a woman, buying something new (even if it is only new to her, like a handbag from a consignment store) makes her *feel* new. One woman had an extremely insightful explanation.

> Getting something new camouflages who we feel like on the inside. That thing is almost a stand-in for *me*. There is something in me that is not good enough, that I want to trade for something that is better. Oh yeah, this cute tunic will improve my life!
>
> What we really want is the actual change. I want to *be* thinner, not just disguise it. But the disguise will work . . . until it doesn't. And then I need more stuff.

Another woman said, "For me it's the house, because that is a representation of *me*. Your home is how you represent yourself. It's like: Look at that pair of chairs at HomeGoods. The chairs I have are scratched and have spit-up on them. But this new pair is fresh, is new, is not the old thing. That makes me *feel* fresh for a while."

Another woman added, "I feel the same way about the kids. I may be exhausted and look terrible, but if I can ensure my child is put together, then I feel like I've got it together."

Multiple women emphasized that the emotional impact was similar even with small purchases. One woman said, "I'm very much a saver. But I get that high, that serotonin release, from spending $3 at yard sales."

It gives her hope of being beautiful. I know it sounds odd that our beautiful wives question this, but they do. Here's how one retired volunteer at the moms convention put it:

I've gained some weight this year, and so when I buy something it's because I think, "Well, this is cute, maybe this will cover up what I'm not liking." A few weeks later I won't like it either. But for now, it is entirely based on the *hope* that it will make me feel better.

This might sound odd to us. (As one of my friends said, "That shirt in *my* closet never looks different. But in *hers*, the same clothes can be great one day and bad the next.") But it also might explain the feelings underneath a pattern many of us have observed!

It is self-care when I'm not feeling cared for. At the moms convention, one hip-looking pastor's wife was very blunt, even as thirty women listened in.

When I shop, I feel loved. My love language is gifts— but this is not just about that. I realize I revert to buying something when something is wrong in the relationship and I can't fix it.

My husband and I are in a stressful season in our ministry. If he hurts me, it is almost like, well, I'm going to make it okay. If I can feel pretty or can go to a nice lunch with a friend or get those cute throw pillows then [smiles delightfully] okay, I'm good!

Some of this is just taking care of myself, and that's not bad. I do think God wants us to enjoy his gifts. But when you look to material things to fix emotional things, you're still empty. You have to go back to the only thing that can fill you up, which is Jesus. And you have to go fix the relationships that are leaving you empty.

In addition to "retail therapy," we heard quite a few other "antidote" feelings and messages women subconsciously pursued:

"I'm worth this." I know it sounds odd, but our amazing wives truly are subconsciously looking for affirmation of their worth. So if your wife is justifying a purchase with "I'm worth it—I am worth getting takeout tonight," it means that if you say no, then her subconscious mind thinks, *You don't feel I'm worth it!* As one woman put it, "I know it's probably irrational, but when my husband says, 'We can't afford this,' I hear, 'We can't afford *you.*'"

Here's how a pediatric nurse explained the "I am worth it" dynamic. "Physiologically, when you get something you love, you have a rush of serotonin. It is so pleasurable to buy a new throw pillow or new flowerpots for the deck. Women are working or driving carpool or doing the laundry and doing the same thing over and over. When I shop, it is a reward for all the thankless stuff I do. By golly, I deserve this mani-pedi."

It allows us to grab together time. This is a big one. Creating together time as a couple or a family—going out to eat, taking vacations, doing things together—is a key way your wife is reassured she is loved *and* a key way for her to build emotional security. The issue is that many (perhaps most!) of those methods involve spending money.

This was a big one for Shaunti when she would want to get Chinese food and I would want to grill the Costco chicken. As she put it, "We've been so busy, and if we cook, it will be an hour of cooking and washing up, and then we have to help the kids with homework, and we won't spend any time together. *Again*. Spending $35 to buy a precious hour of together time as a family? You bet!"

After taking care of others, someone is taking care of me. One mom said, "Why do I like to go out to eat so much? I think it's about being taken care of at a restaurant when I'm not necessarily taken care of at home. I'm a mom, so I'm always taking care of others. But who's taking care of me? Last year when I cracked my nose and went to the hospital, they hovered over me and put warm blankets on me. And I realized it had been a long time since I felt taken care of."

It feels good to be cautious with money. We've spent a lot of time on the spending-money angle, but we should note, again, that many women are savers. Their way of using money as an antidote may look a lot like that of a saving-oriented man, but for very different reasons. One woman told me, "I know it's silly, but I worry about being rejected. Being good with money, watching that savings balance grow, gives me confidence. He likes that too, and I know he's proud of me. And I'm proud of myself. After all . . . confidence is sexy."

My Solution to My Fear Makes Yours Worse

Why is knowing all this so important? It's because the differences between us create one, big, nearly universal problem: *When I try to solve my fear, it makes your fear worse.*

Especially when it comes to building security, we are each trying to *benefit* our partner and our family with our solutions. Yet, ironically, we create several painful and unintended consequences.

Unintended Consequence #1: Seeking "our" type of security makes our partner feel less secure.

Because we care about our spouse and family, we are desperately trying to stay away from the edge of the cliff that we see as most threatening. Surely our partner will be *so grateful* for that, right? And yet, in an irony worthy of a Shakespearean tragedy, the pursuit of "our" type of security makes our partner's fear that much worse. So in response to their fear, our mate pursues "their" security even more.

You can see how this creates a very real but often unseen cycle.

This time, we'll switch the order. For each unintended consequence, Jeff will first tell the guys about the warning bells they need to hear and understand, then Shaunti will share with the women.

His pursuit of financial security can diminish her sense of emotional security.

Guys, we are so motivated to provide, so intensely focused on staying away from the financial cliff, that we can sometimes have blinders on. Our wife might work hard to provide too—but she isn't usually blind to how it is affecting the family.

We make sacrifices to work long hours, giving up time with the family, perhaps missing basketball games and ballet recitals. Maybe we interrupt date nights or family vacations with phone calls or emails. We may take on a new job in retirement instead of doing that long-awaited traveling. We deal with stress and tension from carrying the load, which sometimes spills over onto our family and sometimes just makes us fall asleep in front of the TV during family movie nights.

And we don't realize that it all makes our wives feel more distant from us, and more likely to worry about a lack of emotional security and closeness within the family. We don't like the distance either, of course, but it doesn't loom large in our minds as something that could pull us into dangerous territory. But for her, it does. (Especially because most women already feel stretched to balance enough family time with their *own* work—much less ours!) And it becomes cumulative: As her subconscious concerns grow, she feels every missed family dinner—and every argument between you—that much more acutely.

As one woman put it:

> I think every woman feels unloved when her husband
> spends a lot of time at work and not with the family. I
> do. He's a law enforcement officer, and I know he has a
> stressful job, and I'm proud of him, but it feels like he
> doesn't *want* to connect. I know that can't be true, but
> that's what it feels like.

In her mind, his actions to provide financial security
are sending the family headlong into her greatest fear:
that the family *won't* be okay—that it will pull apart.
And as this woman put it, since there's only so much time
left with the kids at home, they may never really have the
opportunity to pull it back together again.

from
SHAUNTI 🧑 **Her pursuit of emotional security can diminish his**
sense of financial security.

Ladies, let's flip it. As we pursue the security we think
is most important, we don't realize we are making our
man's fear more acute. Back when Jeff and I lived in New
York and he would come wearily home from the law firm
at midnight, I can't tell you how many times I would tear-
fully plead, "Don't you care about me? Can't you just tell
them no?"

Those words strike fear in a man's heart. His brain
instantly cycles through all the monthly bills, the size of
the mortgage or rent payment, the fact that they are still

112

paying off the ER visit from when little Johnny broke his wrist . . . and the consequences of telling his boss "no." He thinks about the fact that the economy could go south or the company could restructure. And within a microsecond, he is standing at the edge of the financial security cliff, staring into the abyss.

Even if we think (as I heard from many wives) *He's one of their top performers! There's no way he's at risk of getting fired*, it sure doesn't feel that way to him. (And, given how easily the market can shift, may not necessarily be true.) On our Decision Analyst survey, among working, married men and women during the prime family years (under age 55 with kids at home), nearly two-thirds of men (compared with just 39 percent of women) said they feel pressure from their spouse to be more engaged with the family—but feel that isn't even an option if they are going to provide for the family!

And now, to top it off, he feels like he's failing as a husband and father, since his wife is unhappy. Men often said they would *love* to be able to work fewer hours but feel caught between the proverbial rock and hard place.

And it's not only our *words* that do that to him, but the actions we take to create emotional security for the family. Creating time together and ensuring our family is happy often involves spending money. It could be a carry-out dinner or the family NASCAR trip; it's great for the family, but (in his mind) creates an even bigger nut to cover. *Even if* you have budgeted and been saving for these things!

The way you solve your worry-window transfers your worry to the other person.

Remember how we handle worry windows differently? Here's another irony: In trying to close our windows, we reach over and open our spouse's.

For a guy, since he can easily close every window but the one about his ability to provide, he does everything he can to keep that window from opening in the first place. Hence the long hours at the office or (for the saver men out there) the twitchiness about going on vacation or going out to eat. For a lot of women, that means he's now transferred his worry to her—she now has an open window about closeness.

Remember that on a woman's side, she can't easily close a window— she often needs to take action to resolve it. And as you saw earlier (Chart 4.6), roughly three out of four women are willing to spend money to do so (such as by taking a child to the doctor). Roughly two-thirds of men in our interviews and informal polls said they would feel like she had closed her window by handing it to him[25] (Chart 4.9).

Unintended Consequence #2: What we naturally do in response to stress and fear triggers the unique insecurity of the other person.

Let's think beyond just money issues for a moment. Our invisible raw nerve of personal insecurity means we are always subconsciously looking for signals about how others feel about us. It means we are jumpy. Our spouses can

Chart 4.9 (MEN): If your wife spends money to close an emotional "window" that is bothering her, does it feel as if she has transferred that open window to you?	
Yes	**67%**
No	**33%**
TOTAL	**100%**

Source: Compilation of event polls, interviews and focus groups 2017–2019.

jab at the raw nerve without having any idea they're doing so—and we can do the same to them.

And what each of us naturally does in response to our fears and stress (including money stress) tends to be one key thing that hits our spouse's raw nerve very directly.

For example, when a man is feeling unappreciated or upset, he often tends to withdraw or get angry—which hits a woman's raw nerve about being secure in and worthy of his love. So after a husband and wife have an emotional argument over breakfast, he might need his space. As he drives away to work, he's setting aside the thought of the argument and concentrating on his job. As *she* drives away, she's wondering, with a twist in her gut, *Are we okay?* She will keep that twist in her gut until she's reassured. He loves his wife, and doesn't even realize her vulnerability exists, much less that it's been triggered and there was a need to reassure her.

So What Do We Do About It?

Well, that was a lot to take in, right? It was for us too. Thankfully, although these fears lie deep within us, there are simple ways of addressing them. Although the *Thriving in Love and Money Discussion Guide* and videos will help you identity what matters most for *you*, we have seen four tips that make a big difference for almost everyone.

Tip 1: Know thyself.

To give our spouses what they need most, we first have to understand our own fears, sensitivities, and reactions—and how they impact our ability to love our partners well.

When you are frustrated about something, ask yourself why. What is stirring the waters? Remember our friend Kyle, who initially had no idea why he was so upset about the Goodwill store? It may take a bit of energy and willingness to figure yourself out.

It helps to ask ourselves questions like:

- "Is it logical to think that I *have* to stay late or I'm going to get fired? Or is that fear talking?"

- "Is it really true that my spouse doesn't care, or is that just what I'm telling myself because I'm hurt?"

- "Is my desire to spend or save right now happening because I'm trying to feel better about myself or close an open window?"

Tip 2: Don't just understand your partner— believe *them when they tell you what matters to them.*

Because our spouse's fears aren't our own, and their solutions aren't our own, it is very, very easy to subconsciously dismiss or downplay them. ("There's no way she really means she would give that up.")

Resist the temptation.

Men: Yes, after months of you being on the new worksite and not seeing your family much, if your wife says she's questioning whether you love her, she means it. It's not just a ploy for attention. If your wife says she'd trade off finances to get more of you, believe that too. As one woman put it:

> My husband thinks I want everything; that I want to have him home more, but that I also secretly want the big lifestyle. He thinks I want to have my cake and eat it too. *No.* I would truly rather have a simple bread we can eat together.

And women: Yes, if your husband worries his job isn't secure, he means that. It may seem irrational to you, but his fear is real. It's not just a ploy to get you to agree to a tighter budget. If he says he would love to be home more and hates being away from you and the kids, believe him.

Tip 3: Show your spouse how to help you in a practical way—and ask how you can help them.

Since your spouse is so different from you: (a) Teach your spouse *how* to help you in a practical way, and (b) ask how *you* can help them.

Remember the opening story of Becky and Tim? When we discussed that story with friends, one husband said, "Sometimes I think we men would love to get off the rat race. But we simply don't know *how.* I'm not sure I would know how to make the specific numbers work in a way that would make my wife and family happy."

So talk about it. If you would love something to change, *show your spouse exactly how it could work, from your perspective*—whether that means living on less money, or prioritizing a dinner out each week for family time.

And ask what *you* can do to help assuage your spouse's fears.

Here are a few rules we heard along the way:

Rule #1: Be specific—especially about what you are willing to change, and what you are hoping for.

Generalities like "I'd love it if we spent more time together on weekends" don't work as well as "I'd love it if you could not work at all on Sundays." And "I'll eat out less" doesn't work as well as "I'll bring lunch twice a week."

Years ago, when I (Shaunti) asked Jeff what gave him that fearful twist in his gut and what I could change, one of the specifics he told me was, "Honestly, it helps if I don't see the shopping bags. I know you're not a crazy spender. I know you know what we can afford. But the shopping bags aren't the issue—the pressure to provide *is*."

Also, be specific about any conditions that are important to you. ("I'm willing to spend more on dinners out, as long as we have the cash and don't have to put them on credit cards.")

Perhaps the biggest disconnect we saw in this entire research project was how hard it was for many men to believe their wives meant it if they said they'd change their lifestyles in return for a better marriage and family. So if you have repeatedly had the same fight about too many hours and not enough family time, stop the cycle. Sit down and get specific about what you both mean. Crunch the numbers. It's a lot harder for a husband to dismiss his wife's comments if she's working from an itemized list and says, "Okay, you'd love that new job with less travel, but it would mean a $15,000 pay cut. I'd love for you to be able to take it, and here are the cuts we could do right off the bat. . . ."

Of course, this works for increasing financial security too. Put on paper things like how much each of you think is necessary to have for emergencies, and what is the specific "right amount" for discretionary spending versus savings.

It's not always easy to come to an agreement. But as long as you are showing what *you* would change, first and foremost, it makes it safer for your spouse to think through their part too.

Rule #2: Be realistic.

Never underestimate your ability to build subconscious barriers against what you *don't* want—or pretend there are no barriers against something you *do* want! Avoid exaggerating the negatives of the other person's position to make it easy to knock down. ("If I make $65,000 instead of $80,000 a year, we'll never be able to vacation again!") But also don't be falsely positive about how easy it will be to do what you are asking. ("Honey, we can easily keep our savings at high levels if you take that more family-friendly job.") Be realistic about *both* sides of the equation: the hard costs and the relational costs.

This includes, as one wife put it, "the cost of *not* doing certain things." She explained, "If we aren't budgeting for family time together—like with Michelle's basketball—we aren't building connection with the kids while they're still at home. We can plan for the financial future—but if we don't attend to the family, we have a probable future relational cost of no family love."

Tip 4: Do things that build your spouse up—and they won't need the antidote as often.

The beauty of how God made us is that, yes, we are different, and with these differences come personal insecurities and fears. And yes, they can be triggered. But they also present opportunities for closeness and intimacy once we understand each other and are tender with our spouse's tender heart.

So have your eyes open to your partner's insecurities, and look for ways to build your spouse up in those areas. (See Chart 4.7 for starting points.) Not only are you being what a spouse should be, but your spouse should need the "antidote" (using money to feel better about themselves) a lot less often.

Here are two things we've found make a big difference to build up men and build up women:[26]

from
SHAUNTI

To build up men. Ladies: We need to hear "I love you," but those words don't have the same impact on a man. For him, they are nice but not necessarily powerful. What *is* powerful is the most important woman in his life saying "thank you" for what he does. "Thank you" says "I *noticed* what you did. And it was *good*. And I *appreciate* it."

from
JEFF

To build up women. Guys, women have far more questions about whether they are loved and lovable, beautiful and special, than we realized. She's wondering that every day, which gives you an opportunity to answer that every day. So when you look at her as she's rocking your little boy to sleep and think, "I can't believe I get to be married to her," don't just think it—*say it*. Send her a text message during the day just to tell her you love her so much. Put your arm around her at church. All those things say, "I would choose you all over again." And if you're upset with her, before you withdraw to clear your mind, say, "I need space, but I want you to know *we're okay*."

Counter Fear by Trusting God

This is the longest chapter in the book, and we've talked about all sorts of emotional issues and factors, all of which thread back to one thing: fear. In our view, the solution ties back to one factor as well. Let's wrap up this discussion with a thought shared by our friend Danielle:

Really, all of this has to do with figuring out why we're unsettled to begin with. The root is fear. And how do we combat fear? With *truth*. The truth that we can trust God when we're worried. When we're feeling worthless.

When we got the news that Kyle's company was being acquired and there would be layoffs, the anxiety started . . . and then we said "No." We are going to tell ourselves the truth that God cares and we can trust him.

5 Show Me the Money—and Then Let Me Handle It

Why our tendency toward independence may not be so liberating after all

Insight #3—We resist being fully one in our marriage—and it is coming out in our finances.

In our interviews with an incredibly diverse array of people, over and over we heard comments like these:

- "We have a joint account, but I also have one that's just mine. When we got married, my mom said, 'You never know what might happen, so you should set something aside just in case.'"

- "Amazon Prime is our big money drain. I ask my wife, 'Why do you spend money on these things?'

She says, 'I *tried* to get the Amazon package off the front porch before you got home.'"

- "He has tons of student loans. He doesn't want me to have to pay for those because they were his decision."

- "We are on each other's bank accounts, but in practice we only use our own. The rent comes out of mine; the utilities come out of hers. We have a joint savings that we each pay into, but other than that, we tend to do our own thing. It cuts down on a lot of arguing."

- "My husband offered to help when I had to re-place a timing belt, but I said I could cover it with my pension money. I don't want to feel like I can't handle it myself."

What do these remarks have in common?

In each case, the speaker is resisting being truly *one* with their spouse. Instead of seeing marriage as two people who have been inextricably (and, as the Bible describes it, *supernaturally*) bonded for life—and thus two people who need to work to eliminate every obstacle to becoming one team—these spouses hold themselves back in some way. And it is reflected in how they handle money.

Some may think, *I would never do that.* But the truth is, we all resist being one in our marriages in *some* way. It is the nature of us imperfect, selfish creatures. Trying to snag the Amazon package off the porch before our spouse gets home is just a subtle symptom of the same self-protective, underlying tension that drives other couples to separate their finances completely.

Ironically, as we try to protect ourselves we risk creating the very outcome we are trying to avoid! In our research for *The Surprising Secrets of Highly Happy Marriages*, we found that those who maintain some independence as a way to protect themselves (like having a bank account on the side), were more than twice as likely to be in a so-so or struggling marriage.[27]

By contrast, the happiest couples fought the temptation (or advice!) to draw a line between "yours" and "mine." They fully shared everything, holding nothing back. Bank accounts, credit cards, user names, passwords, PIN numbers, emails, text messages—they shared it all.

Now, how those thriving couples *arranged* their shared money and information was as diverse as they were—many of them used different accounts or had different credit cards out of sheer convenience. But each could access everything.

(The only exceptions, beyond the scope of this book, are where a spouse is abusive or has a true disorder, such as a gambling addiction. In such a situation, seek out qualified counseling and pastoral care immediately, since you likely *will* need strict boundaries and separate accounts while addressing it.)

125

Why do we resist being a team in money?

Everyone goes into marriage wanting closeness. Deep down, we *want* to be a united team with someone who will always have our back. Someone who will love and appreciate us no matter what.

The problem is, we also want our own way. Which doesn't exactly help create that one-team unity.

We actually want our own way in every area, but it's particularly obvious with money. Jesus famously pleaded with his listeners to stop focusing on building up things of earthly value, and focus on what matters for eternity: "For where your treasure is, there your heart will be also."[28]

> What we do with money always reveals the heart—and steers the heart.

In other words: When someone looks at how we handle money, they'll see what we value. What we do with money always reveals the heart—and steers the heart. It shows what we are *really* thinking and feeling better than almost anything else.

The Unity-Busters

There are many ways to arrange finances—but they don't matter as much as the intent and heart beneath

126

them. Now, when unity and oneness is the goal, certain "best practices" tend to arise—in particular, ensuring that each partner has full access to all finances. But even among couples that *do* want unity and are striving toward oneness, even among those who share all finances **and** try to be "all in," certain subconscious thoughts, feelings, and actions can still sneak in. Based on extensive analysis of the Dynata survey, roughly 80 percent of married couples have meaningful indicators of a lack of oneness—whether they know it or not. (See Chart 5.1.) In fact, this mindset of wanting our own way so sneakily saturates our hearts that Chuck Cowan's analysis of the Dynata survey found it is what *most* explains the attitudes and actions of the survey-takers as a whole.[29]

Although these are all intertwined, here are seven unity-busting thoughts. As you read, be honest with yourself and note which sneaky thoughts sometimes cross *your* mind.

Chart 5.1: **We resist being one.** (Among married couples)	
Those who give in to the temptation to not be "all in" with money:	**80%**[30]
Those who successfully are "all in" with money:	**20%**
TOTAL	**100%**
	Source: Analysis of Dynata survey.

Awareness is the first step toward rooting out a damaging thought or habit and choosing a path of "oneness" instead.

Unity-Buster #1: "I want to do what I want to do."

The greatest barrier to being one team is that each of us kinda just wants to do what we want to do, without being accountable to our partner. On the Dynata survey, 67 percent of respondents admitted they may not want to talk about money because "I just want to be able to handle money the way I want to handle money" (Chart 5.2). And to some degree, we are always either fighting that temptation or giving in to it. We heard several common feelings underneath the surface.

Chart 5.2: There are many reasons why someone might find talking about money difficult at times. [Do you feel . . . ?]	
"Candidly, I just want to be able to handle money the way I want to handle money."	
Yes definitely/sometimes	**67%**
No	**33%**
TOTAL	**100%**
	Source: Dynata survey.

"After all . . . it's my money."

We'll talk about this more in chapter 7, but underlying many of these feelings is the subconscious (or overt) feeling that money is "mine" or "yours," not "ours." And I should be able to do what I want with what is mine! This may be the reason that 47 percent of respondents on the Dynata survey said that, however else they arranged their finances, they did have a personal bank or credit card account their partner could not access.

Of course, this also institutionalizes *not* being a team, solidifying expectations that may not be unified when unity is most needed. (For example, who "owns" the money when one spouse stays home with the kids? When one person's investment account made more money by the time of retirement?)

"I don't want someone telling me 'no.'"

Listen to how a thirty-something woman processed this feeling:

> To be candid, I don't want to ask my husband things like, "Hey, I want to spend this amount getting my hair done." Because then there's an opportunity for him to say no. And if he says no, then what? Whereas, if it's kind of hidden, and it's done, he can't tell me no.

"If I/we can afford it, why should I not do what I want to do?"

One young man next to me on a flight summarized what a lot of us are probably also thinking: *And why should I have to pull back anyway?* He told me he and his partner had just broken up. He said, "I always wrestled with the fact that I've worked hard to make a good salary, and why should I have to stay in a Motel 6 when we go on vacation just because my partner feels like a Marriott costs too much?"

"After all, my partner is doing what they want to do"

It's easy to justify doing what we want to do when we see our spouse doing the same thing! As one woman laughingly put it, "If he's not going to give me access to his account, why should I give him access to mine? I'm not going to push the issue, because I'm making my own money."

Secret shopping/secret savings

Trying to keep purchases out of our spouse's view (which 37 percent of Dynata survey-takers confess to) is an easy sign that we're trying to do what we want—and keep it from our spouse. But doing what we want is not just about spending. Multiple people said something like what we heard from this nurse:

We set up a joint account right away, but I really, really wanted a separate account too. So I set up a savings account that he doesn't know about. Not because I'm "trying to hide money" but because he simply isn't a saver. I needed savings he can't touch.

There's nothing inherently dangerous about spending a certain amount on hotels, or even creating a set-aside savings account. (One husband chuckled as he said, "My wife is a saver, but both of us know I can't save a dime. So together we decided that a certain amount of each paycheck goes into an account that *only* she can access. Problem solved!") Where it pulls people apart is when one person does what they want regardless of what their spouse thinks.

As this woman regretfully described, doing so can create far greater problems than the annoyance of having to compromise or give up what we want:

Money was a huge factor in our marriage falling apart. I would make a lot of decisions without talking to Trevor. Looking back, I realize I must have really made him feel insignificant. I was afraid he would disagree with my decisions, so I just wouldn't give him the chance. Like, I needed a new car, and when my mom died I took the money she left me and went car shopping. I loved the way one drove, so I bought it. Trev made a comment that he wished I had taken him to see it. But I thought it was my money, so I was going to spend it the way I wanted to.

131

We started marriage with separate checking accounts for convenience, and we just kept going like that. And it made it too easy to live very separate lives.

Unity-Buster #2: I want to be in control.

Ultimately, we want to be in control because we want the power to do what *we* want to do! As one woman put it, "The idea of being controlled is emotional. I'm not fighting to buy shoes. I'm fighting for the freedom to get them when I want to!"

But there are several other reasons we want control, and several ways it plays out.

"The other person might do it wrong."

Many of us have to admit that a main reason we want to make the decisions is because we think we know best and our spouse might do it "wrong."

One woman was very honest that her tendency to control was one reason her spouse backed off on money issues. She said, "I know I have a double standard with Rob. I have a driver personality, and if I see a trend in our investments that might cause a problem, I want to get ahead of it. It's frustrating that he is slow and steady. But when he *does* take initiative, I end up saying, 'Eh, that wasn't right.' So of course he doesn't want to step up! It makes me nervous, but I know I need to compromise, and not always be in control."

One engaged woman recognized how negative her assumptions had been:

Her: We did a Prepare-Enrich assessment in our premarital counseling and found that we have almost all strengths except in the area of finances, where we are way off. I'm more conservative, and he's idealistic. He'll regularly pick up the tab for lunch with a friend. He doesn't see things the same way. I'm not trying to be frugal or controlling, I'm trying to help him see that you can't spend everything you have. He simply doesn't see it as a problem. It comes from his generous heart, which is why I was attracted him in the first place. But I'm also trying to help him realize we can't live like that.

Jeff: Is your hope that with enough history and education he can come to see things the way you do?

Her: That would be my hope.

Shaunti: So there's a "right way" and a "wrong way"?

Her: (Pause) I guess I've been thinking that, and he needs to get on board with my way of seeing it. (Pause) But now that you ask, I see I may need to rethink and maybe there are shades of gray.

Shaunti: If you were in *his* brain, what would you say he is thinking? "This more idealistic way is right because . . ."

Her: I think he would say "I'm generous, and isn't that
what God wants?" He'd be thinking, of course I'm
going to buy lunch for my friend. That's how I can
bless someone else. He would say we aren't guaran-
teed tomorrow and we have to trust day by day.

**We make sharing control a bigger deal than it has
to be.**

Sometimes we make giving up control into a much
bigger issue than it is. In the Orlando airport, I (Shaunti)
struck up a conversation with a group of colleagues
heading home from a business trip. Upon hearing that
several of his co-workers allowed their spouses to be the
one tracking the expenses, one man shook his head.

I could never relinquish control of knowing what is going
on. That terrifies me. You could find yourself in a bad
situation so fast. My wife feels the same, so she has her
own account too. We've been married eighteen months.
She doesn't want me to have control over her and vice
versa. That's never going to change.

This man and his wife explicitly see unity in marriage
as terrifying because (in their minds) giving up control
means allowing someone to control them and keep them
in the dark.

And yet, as another woman described, they are letting
fear create an imaginary problem that usually doesn't exist.

134

"When I feel like there's an imbalance of power in a relationship, there's this fear that someone is going to have control over me. Which I realize is stupid. If I'm going to have a good marriage, *of course* I have to share control over my life!'"

We might add that it also is not the same thing as "not knowing what is going on." The couples we talked to who seemed most well-balanced and happy in their love and money journey could access all the financial information they wanted to, and—more importantly—actively talked about money so both partners always *did* know what was going on.

Even when control is needed, it has to be handled respectfully.

Sometimes there's a legitimate reason why one partner needs to establish more control. Although we can't deal with actual addictions here, we did cross paths with several people who simply needed their partner to help them with unhealthy tendencies toward excessive spending or saving. (It is important to seek qualified counsel to understand *how* to establish respectful boundaries without triggering greater problems.)

Although this often involves overspending, we also met multiple people with unhealthy tendencies toward *not* spending, who clamped down more and more as their spouses tried to get them to "have a life." One wife was so obsessive about getting out of debt that her husband had to take over the finances to allow the family to breathe. She responded to her loss of control by telling her twice-monthly coffee-shop book club (which she loved) that she could no longer join them because it meant spending $5 each month for coffee.

Putting things in perspective: What is most important?

We spoke with many couples who realized that jockeying for control was hurting the relationship, which was far more precious than their money would ever be. One couple described their awakening to this truth:

Her: We've both had spouses leave us before. And both of us used to have this knee-jerk desire to hold onto things. Like, deciding who would pay the bills.

Him: If you're paying the bills, you have the power: You're the one who knows exactly where the money is going. So for a while we did it together, but it's hard to have two people do the spreadsheet! It was getting bad. Which is when we pulled back and said, "This is hurting *us*. Nothing is worth that."

Her: What should I be *most* afraid of? I am more afraid of losing us than I am afraid of losing power over money.

Him: What we have now is precious. Once we keep that in mind, it is very easy to put money in its proper context. Now she does the monthly bills and I do the investing and we're both happy with what we're doing.

We're not really in control anyway.

Many of the successful couples we talked to had come to a big-picture perspective based on their faith. One wife wrestled with giving up control after her husband lost his job and he said he might as well take over the finances since he had extra time.

I had to confront it: Do I have faith or not? Honestly, I felt like God was taking me on this journey of releasing control in general. With the kids, with every area.

And then suddenly being in financial hardship, I saw I really don't have control over this life anyway. So I'm going to trust my husband and ultimately trust the Lord.

Unity-Buster #3: Lack of trust

Not surprisingly, the core reason we want to control things—and avoid being one in general—often comes down to a subconscious lack of trust. Or even a conscious one! In our Dynata survey, when we asked those who sometimes use separate bank accounts their reasons for doing so, nearly *one-quarter of married respondents* said, "We're not yet at a place in our relationship or financial health where we should have fully merged accounts."

Many of us might think, *Of course I trust my spouse!* After all, almost everyone trusts their spouse to be "honest" with money—to not embezzle all the marital assets and then split.

But there are several sneaky ways that, when it comes to money, we may not *actually* trust our partner, even if we "feel" like we trust him or her.

"I don't trust you to care about what I care about."

This is essentially what chapter 3 is about, right? We can *tell* that our partner doesn't always understand or value what we value—so we hold on tightly to our ability to do what *we* care about. This is why I (Shaunti) instinctively want to avoid a joint budget: I struggle with trusting that Jeff will respect my desire to allocate money for Chinese takeout. And why he (understandably) doesn't trust me to care about his desire to have a budget!

"I don't trust you to handle money well."

Or as one young wife told us: "I want our finances to reflect that we really are one in marriage. But I still get nervous. Justin isn't a crazy spender, but he isn't nearly as strict about sticking to our budget as I am. If I'm honest, in the back of my mind, part of me is thinking, 'Is this realistically going to help him save more?' Or once we build up the savings account is he going to see it as 'Oh look! More money!'"

"I don't trust us to make it."

No one goes into marriage expecting to fail. But usually when someone kept money their spouse couldn't access it was because they felt the need for a just-in-case backup plan.

But they usually didn't word it that way. They would say things like, "After all, who knows what might happen?" Or, "The way things are today, it's just better to be prepared to take care of the kids if I need to." Nearly everyone who took this step implied they would be foolish *not* to.

As we said earlier, though, the reality is the opposite: Those actions to "be safe" can cause the very problems couples are trying to protect themselves from. One couple who had come back from the brink of divorce to eventually have a thriving marriage told us that trying to protect yourselves "creates a wedge. There is intimacy not shared. . . . If you can't be vulnerable enough to trust your spouse in that area, then there's going to be weakness in other areas of your relationship."[31]

Trust creates trust.

Thankfully, though, the reverse is also true. If we are willing to communicate and work toward mutual understanding, there are great opportunities for building trust. As one wife described, "After thirty years of marriage, it's like we've been to the front lines. We had to decide whether to rely on each other or to charge up the hill alone. We couldn't focus on who made what mistakes. We had to show each other, 'I have your back.'"

Unity-Buster #4: I want to be independent, take care of myself, and not owe anyone anything— so no one can hurt me.

Many of us find ourselves wanting to keep a little bit of independence, a little bit of a wall, so we don't get hurt. Or because, we think, I'm perfectly capable of taking care of myself.

The problem is, marriage is designed *for us to take care of each other.* To lean on and rely on each other. There is no way to become fully one without that step.

Although this unity-buster occurs among all demographic groups, and is actually slightly more prevalent among young men, we heard a great deal about this temptation among young women.

This was revealed in a dialogue from a focus group with six youngish couples (all under age forty) at a church on the West Coast, pondering the reasons for this particular temptation. This is a long dialogue, but we felt it was so insightful we didn't want to cut it further. (As you'll see, the men were mostly conspicuously silent.)

Jada: When we got married, Scott said he *wanted* to cover a lot of the larger bills, like paying off my student loans. But I have been so resistant. If he takes care of that, I'll feel like I owe him. Even though he's my *husband!* I feel like if he helps me, I'm in a subordinate position.

Mari: I feel like, "I don't need your help because I know I'm capable." And yes, I am capable—but that doesn't allow for the gift of my man wanting to help. To say, "It's okay, I don't *have* to do it myself." There's definitely a level of pride. But it's okay to ask for help. It's okay to receive help. And if I'll let myself relax, it feels good to know my spouse is willing to help and that we're in this together. I wonder why I shy away from that?

Shellie: I think it's the Beyoncé effect or something. We grew up hearing, "Girl, you got this. You don't need a man!" You need to be strong, which means being independent. But then in church, you hear: You're supposed to be completely blended together.

Jada: I've always had this wall. Like, if a husband comes along, he's a bonus, but I've got myself together and I'm good and I don't need anyone to help me. I'm sure it's a defense mechanism. I'm conditioned to protect myself. Which is crazy, because when I have kids, I have this secret dream to be a stay-at-home mom for a while. But I feel like I absolutely shouldn't have that dream.

Shellie: There's this deep-rooted fear of being vulnerable. It's difficult to receive. Because if you're receiving, you're not in control.

Jada: The fear of allowing someone to fully take care of you. Because then what happens if they're not there?

Scott: It's understandable that that fear is there. In our generation a lot of guys, once they find out their girl is pregnant, just take off. My wife has a lot of friends who are single mothers, and it hurts to see that, you know? These women are forced to raise kids by themselves. They *have* to be independent.

Jacqueline: And then the kids learn independence from their mother. My daughter's nineteen on Sunday. She's just like what I've raised: "I'm going to take care of myself. No man is going to take care of me." She saw what happened when her dad left, so it's self-preservation. There's an inner strength when you know you've got this and you don't have to rely on somebody else. The problem is, we're strong, but we can be lonely.

Shellie: Let's be honest—it's not just self-protective. I think there's a haughtiness to it.

Like, "I make my money. I'm going to spend it how I want to spend it." See what I mean? It's like I'm taking the power away from him to tell me no. These are all bad things, but I think I feel them. [Looks ruefully at her husband] I admire my husband so much for putting up with me while I figure this out.

After hearing many comments like these, we began asking men, privately, what they thought.

What we heard, over and over, was captured perfectly by one thirty-something man we interviewed on his own, who had been living with his girlfriend for eighteen months. She insisted on equally splitting all the bills, even though he wished she would let him help her sometimes. He explained: "She doesn't want to feel like she needs anyone." How did he feel about that? "I'm totally neutral," he said.

Yet near the end of our long interview he mentioned several times that he wished she would be more vulnerable and willing to accept financial help. And when I (Shaunti) hesitantly said, "It doesn't sound like you're actually 'neutral,'" I was astonished to see his eyes get red.

"Yeah. It does hurt a little bit," he said. "It hurts because it means I'm not good enough. I'm not where I need to be, financially, or as a partner. If I was what she needed, she wouldn't have that need for independence."

Unity-Buster #5: It's easier and quicker to just do it myself.

A parallel to wanting control is the sense that "it will be too much work to get to oneness, so it's easier to just do things myself."

As we saw in chapter 2, plenty of mutants—er, people—actually look forward to talking about money and putting together budgets. But for the rest of us, doing things separately can be tempting just because it feels easier than talking, connecting, and coming to an agreement without undue strife. On the Dynata survey, among married couples who said they sometimes use separate bank accounts, 42 percent do so to avoid tense money conversations (Chart 5.3). Of course the trap is that this practically ensures we will *never* be able to talk about it!

Unity-Buster #6: My spouse shouldn't have to pay for my debt.

On the Dynata survey, among married people who sometimes used separate bank accounts and had consumer or

---

Chart 5.3: Among those who use separate accounts at times:

"When we try to discuss money, things get awkward and tense and we end up having conflict. Having separate accounts helps us to avoid all that."   **42%**

Source: Dynata survey.

---

student debt to manage, more than *one-third* (38 percent) said that one reason for the separate accounts was so one spouse didn't have to pay for the other's debt (Chart 5.4).

Chart 5.4. Among those who use separate accounts at times:

"We have separate accounts so one spouse is not obligated to pay the other person's debt."   **38%**

Source: Dynata survey. (Among married individuals with separate accounts, who have consumer/student debt)

Especially among those in their first decade out of school, it was extremely common for us to hear discussions like this one:

> *Lexi:* When we got married, Austin's financial situation was a lot better than mine. I recognized I was hesitant to join our stuff because I have student loans and I feel like that's my responsibility. I didn't want to combine finances because I didn't want him to have to cover what I accumulated during my singleness.

> *Cherise:* I was the same way. I had loans and I'm like, "Once he sees what I have, he's going to want a divorce!" I made it this mountain in my mind. But then when we talked about it, he was so loving and accepting. And that's when I realized what was

going on in my head wasn't really about the money. I was afraid of him saying, essentially, "I love you less because of this money thing." And his reaction helped us connect more and to build trust because he broke down a wall of fear that I didn't even realize I had. [Pause] Think about it: Would you have the same hesitation if the student loans were *his?*

Lexi: I think I would figure out how we could work together to get it done. But because it was my debt *he* was paying off, it was a knee-jerk thing. I felt like it would put us out of balance if he was simply taking care of me.

As Lexi began to realize, although wanting to spare your spouse your student loans often comes from a heart of generosity, running under the surface is the same damaging hesitation about becoming one.

Unity-Buster #7: Leaning on a parent or family instead of a spouse

A final sneaky way we resist being one is by prioritizing parents or family in certain money decisions, instead of our spouse. As one woman said, "He keeps sending money to his family in Mexico. I love them, but there has to be a limit. I told him I was tired of me working to give money to his family! He said, 'Family comes first.' I told him, *this* is your family! You answer to this family first, not *that* family!"

While many younger couples appreciate a little financial guidance from a parent, that only works if the spouse is in full agreement that the guidance is needed. Otherwise, it becomes a unity-buster. Here's how one woman in her late twenties described it:

> We are separated right now, and it's because of money. Long story short, we were car shopping and pregnant with our second child, so we needed to save. But Dante has never had anything in his life and wanted all the extras, and the dealer saw him as an easy mark. We could afford a $250 payment and ended up with a brand-new car with a $565 payment. I tried to tell him I thought it was a bad idea, and that my dad thought it was a bad idea. But then it was a pride thing, and Dante said I needed to trust him. Now he knows he made a really bad decision. But he won't say he was wrong.
>
> I talked to Dad about it and the best decision really was to turn the car in. So I did it, even though Dante didn't want me to and said it would hurt our credit. And anyway . . . that's why we're separated.

Dante made a very poor decision and ignored his wife's cautions. Yet we suspect that much of the unhealthy dynamic was exacerbated by Dante sensing his wife respected her father more than she respected him. He probably also found it even harder to admit his failure, knowing that it would mean admitting it not just to his wife but to her father.

147

Although his poor decision is entirely on him, we suspect he would have been far more willing to *listen* to his wife if he knew she wholeheartedly supported and believed in him overall.

Unity-Building Factors

Thankfully, many couples recognize the tendencies that could pull them apart and try to come together in money instead. Those who do are far more likely to also be happy in their finances and their marriage.[32]

One particular couple was a great case study. Aaron and Kelly married in their mid-thirties. They were very different, had their own ways of handling money, and valued their independence . . . and yet they also knew a great marriage required coming together as one. Listen to how Kelly describes her thought process:

Before we got married, I would spend all my extra money on clothes and creating a beautiful home. But he spent all his money on traveling and doing triathlons around the world. For him, a home is entirely about convenience: He *really* wanted to have little or no commute. But in Southern California, living close to work usually means having a place that is small and run-down!

When we got married, we ended up buying a nice condo a long way from his work, which was *not* what he would have done. But it was so important to me, and we're partners: If it's important to you, it's important to me. But as soon as we got the condo, I planned to decorate it and do all this stuff! But he just wanted to start saving money. I had to think: This is not about me! He gave up his house near work for me, and I just have to get over myself. So I partially decorated, not fully. It was a grieving process. And for him, he had to cut travel by half so he wasn't gone all the time. We made a commitment to be partners.

But that also meant I had to be willing to work on a budget. I'm still me, but I'm not on my own anymore.

"I'm still me, but I'm not on my own anymore." That's a great summary of something each of us needs to remember in order to thrive in love and money. We identified five unity-building factors that are important to that outcome.

Unity-Builder #1: Be aware of the tendency to resist being one—and take purposeful steps to counter it.

We all have a sneaky tendency to want to do what we want to do, to be in control, and so on. And we can't counter it until we see it for what it is, call it out, and take action to be one team instead.

When I (Shaunti) pull into the garage with more purchases from Costco than Jeff was expecting and see his car isn't there, I'm relieved. I have to see that for what it is: I'm relieved because now I can get away with not confessing I got that extra little space heater or that bag that was on *such* a good sale—even though I'd promised to cut down on spending. To build unity, I have to tell him that I made a judgment call—but I'm totally willing to return these things if he'd prefer it.

And when I (Jeff) have a tendency to say, "Since you got all those extra things, I will do without my trip to the eye doctor, even though I need new glasses," I have to see it for what it is: a desire to control things by playing the martyr—as well as "punish" Shaunti for spending more.

Unity-Builder #2: Recognize what is most important—and act like it is.

Very few people say having a lot of money is more important than a great marriage. Yet, when we resist being one team with money, we are essentially acting like money is more important!

> Every day, we have to decide to act as the team we want to be, even when we don't feel like it.

Every day, we have to decide to act as the team we want to be, even when we don't feel like it. In our finances we have to work toward and be willing to compromise for what is best for our *marriage*—not for what we individually want or value.

As we'll discuss shortly, we also have to dismantle any systems we've put in place that are keeping us apart. That could mean something big like prenuptial agreements or secret bank accounts, or something seemingly minor like hiding Walmart receipts. If we care about our marriage more than money, we have to set aside fear and eliminate those marriage-killing factors that, in reality, we should fear far more.

As one newlywed put it: "Finances are a big part of life. But trust is more foundational than finances."

Unity-Builder #3: Believe the best of your spouse's intentions toward you—and look for evidence of that.

It will always be hard to become one team unless you let yourself believe what is almost certainly true: Your spouse deeply cares about you and has your best interests at heart—even when they handle money in a way that frustrates you.

In our *Surprising Secrets of Highly Happy Marriages* research, we discovered that with very, very few exceptions, most spouses truly do care about their mate—and believing that in the face of legitimate hurt (since we all hurt each other at times) was the most foundational step toward a thriving marriage.

One of the best ways to practice this is to constantly look for the good in your spouse when it comes to money, and for evidence that your spouse cares about you. You'll find it everywhere. For example, Aaron and Kelly had a high level of goodwill and trust because they had each *noticed* the sacrifices the other made.

It is also crucial to note that budgets, with targets, are *necessary* if we're going to notice our spouse's generosity! Many couples said that if they didn't have a budget, if each partner spent money on anything they wanted, they'd never understand what certain decisions were costing the other.

Unity-Builder #4: Create joint ownership and awareness in your budget and finances.

If there are things you've been holding back, now is the time to bring everything into the open. Again, there's no one right way to arrange your finances. For example, some couples use different accounts or credit cards for convenience. But as long as there aren't extraordinary mitigating circumstances, both of you should be fully aware of and have access to everything. Some of you will have done this from the beginning. For others, this will be a huge step of faith. If your spouse takes that step of trust, honor it. Show them how thankful you are. And if you need someone to help you work through these issues, reach out to a qualified counselor or coach who shares the value of getting you to full transparency.

Thankfully, dismantling any systems that pull us apart will usually build trust and closeness. One young husband described how being forced to have transparency in a different area (when his wife discovered his porn problem), spilled over into transparency and trust in every area—including money:

> As we were going into counseling, I was changing to a much lower-paying job. We originally had a lot of conflict and disconnect when we made financial decisions. But because we were coming together in our marriage, we didn't want something hidden in *any* area. So we started opening up about money too. We had much less money, but much more peace of mind and happiness in our marriage. Bringing everything out of darkness has literally changed our lives.

Ironically, allowing for each partner's individuality in what they value appears to be a key to creating oneness. Over and over, we heard from thriving couples the same idea we shared in chapter 3: They allocate a monthly amount of money that each partner can spend on whatever they value, without having to check in with the other person. The key is allowing *individuality* without an unhealthy mindset of *independence*.

Unity-Builder #5: Trust God.

We know readers differ on matters of faith. But we believe that trusting God is the only real foundation for how to counter selfishness and fear, build transparency, and trust one another, especially when we get very practical and real with money issues.

As one woman put it, "It is hard for me, sometimes, to trust my husband since I know he will make different choices than I would. That's when I force myself to say: I *can* trust God. And since God asks me to trust my husband, and I know my husband is a good guy who is trying his best, I believe God will honor that. Even if my husband makes mistakes. [Laughs] Or what I *see* as mistakes."

One man had some great advice: "As you are about to take any action step on money—whether that's hiding the Amazon packages, or depositing money in savings that your spouse doesn't know about—stop and imagine Jesus literally beside you. Our motivation must be, 'Whatever you do [how you handle the Amazon packages!], do it all for the glory of God.'"[33]

How You Handle Money Will Change Your Heart

It is true that how we handle money shows what is in our hearts. But it works the other way as well: Purposefully changing how you handle money, focusing on what matters most, will change your heart.

All of us have selfishness inside. If that is allowed to grow, it will show up in how we handle money. But as we force ourselves toward true oneness in marriage, we have to confront these issues head on. We have to be vulnerable. To trust. To talk.

Exposing ourselves completely to our spouse may seem risky. But the rewards are great.

6 What We Have Here Is a Failure to Communicate

How different ways of thinking and listening cause conflict instead of connection

> Insight #4—When dealing with money, our different wiring for processing and communication makes us clash instead of connect.

Desiree and Sal were not having a good evening. For weeks, Desiree had been preparing to host a birthday dinner bash for her younger sister, cooking and freezing food in advance so on the day of the party she could pop it in the oven. Sal had been cleaning the yard and fixing up the house. The big day was on Sunday, and on Wednesday Desiree pulled a can of Diet Coke from the refrigerator and realized, to her horror . . . it wasn't very cold.

Desiree, an analytical sort, began talking through their options. Should they get a repairman? The consultation would cost something, but fixing the fridge would likely total a few hundred dollars instead of $1,000 or more to buy a new one. On the other hand, their neighbors the Maxwells spent $350 repairing their refrigerator last year only to have it die a few months later. Maybe they should just suck it up, save the repairman cost, and buy a new fridge. In which case they should probably look online for sales and go to Home Depot tonight. After all, the party was Sunday and who knew how long all the frozen appetizers, casseroles, and desserts would last?

"What do you think?" Desiree asked Sal.

"I don't know," he said in a vague tone, looking away.

After a pause, she said, "Well, we have to figure this out. What are you thinking as a starting point?"

"I don't know. I have to think about it." Sal started to walk away.

Desiree followed, her voice rising with frustration. "We don't have time to think about it! We only have two hours before Home Depot closes. Or we should call the repair people right away and get on their schedule for tomorrow!" Seeing Sal's blank face, she said in anger, "I am really worried about this! It took me days to get all that food prepared and frozen! Should we at least start by calling the repair people?"

"Go ahead, if you think that's what we should do."

"Well, what are *you* thinking we should do?! I can't read your mind!"

Now Sal sounded frustrated too. "I told you, I don't know!" He kept walking away. "I need to check whether my client emailed me back. Let me think. Let's talk about this later."

Before He Says/She Says

Does that scenario sound at all familiar? When Sal and Desiree shared that incident, they described it as a "problem with communication."

But actually . . . it wasn't.

We all know that couples often have very different communication styles. But many of the problems that seem to be about communication actually stem from differences in *processing.* Specifically, how we think through decisions about money—and everything else!

They are also often a sign of problems with *listening.*

If we want great communication around money, first we need to *understand and honor our differences in processing and listening.* We need to work *with* what our spouse needs rather than against it. If we do, we'll be much better able to address each other's communication needs, which are different in every person and every marriage. (We'll also be better able to address the money feelings and factors we need to communicate *about,* which is what we cover in the other chapters!)

These communication differences are the other topic that appears to be quite gender-related (in addition to the discussion of fear and security in chapter 5). In this case there's a strong tie to key differences in brain wiring, although there are also plenty of exceptions.

We'll approach this primarily from a male-female perspective, but as you read, identify which processing and listening patterns seem most applicable to you and your spouse, regardless of gender. (You can work through those questions in the curricula that goes along with this book.)

Our Way of Thinking Things Through May Clash with Our Partner's

Sal and Desiree's refrigerator dilemma is a perfect example of how men and women tend to need different processes for thinking through and talking about important money decisions, how this can cause conflict, and how we often don't realize what is actually going on. Thankfully, once we understand this we can create ground rules for how to handle discussions about money that will often lead to much greater harmony and connection.

Let's cover four surprising truths about processing—and the related topic of listening. As before, Shaunti will share with the women about how men tend to think, and Jeff will talk to the men about how women tend to think. (Remember, many will find themselves processing in a way more common to the opposite sex.)

Surprising Truth #1: Male and female brains tend toward opposite processing styles.

Okay, maybe that isn't so surprising. We've all seen it in action—but we may not have understood what we were seeing!

Perhaps in part because of differences in brain wiring,* women tend to think things through by talking them through, while men tend to think things through internally. Here's a simplified look at some of the neurobiological reasons that appear to play a role.[34]

When a baby is conceived, all fetuses start out using a female template for the brain. But if the baby has a Y chromosome and is thus designed to be male, at about four to six weeks in utero a testosterone burst triggers the development of male genitals, which then begin pushing out testosterone. This radically changes the developing brain.[35] For those babies designed to be female, in the absence of that testosterone push, the brain continues to develop as it started.[36]

As the fetus, and later the baby, grows, the male brain develops more gray matter (the computing matter[37]) and has more gray matter activity, while the female brain develops more white matter (the connecting, networking

---

* For the sake of a basic explanation, we are simplifying complex neuroscience that is still developing; there may also be other factors responsible for the common patterns observed between men and women. For more detail, see the books and articles referenced in the citations.

matter) between the two hemispheres of the brain.[38] The female brain also ends up with far more extensive connections *within* the brain hemispheres, whereas the male brain has fewer, more "modular" connections.[39] Further, the female brain appears to be wired for, as one study put it, "a female advantage in verbal processing," including articulating (and recalling) emotions.[40]

In an extremely simplified, layman's way of looking at it, we might say that the male brain tends to process inputs using large, isolated supercomputers that aren't particularly connected—which may be one reason why men tend to think of one thing at a time, go into it very deeply, perhaps act on what they decided, and then move on to the next thing. We might say that the female brain processes inputs using many more smaller computers that are networked together and working at the same time (including a strong network with the verbal centers). This may be one reason why women can multitask on many thoughts or feelings and talk about them at the same time.[41]

> In the end, both the male and female brain arrive at the same processing power, but they get there in different ways.

In the end, both the male and female brain arrive at the same processing power, but they get there in different ways. All of which leads to several key consequences when the average man and woman have to process a money decision about buying a refrigerator!

Here's how it works.

Men go underground to think things through.

Ladies, where we as women often find it natural to think things through by talking, men are exactly the opposite. For most men (although certainly not all) it is actively difficult to think through an important decision (money or otherwise) by talking about it. They can do it if they need to or want to, just as we can think something through internally. But for seven in ten men on our Decision Analyst survey (69 percent), their predisposition is to go underground instead; to silently think through all the options and all the ramifications of those options—and absolutely, positively *not* talk about it with us until they've done the internal chess match and figured out what they are thinking (Chart 6.1).

This is what was happening in Sal as he and Desiree tried to figure out what to do about the refrigerator. Like many of us, Desiree wanted to know right away what Sal was thinking, and like many men in that situation, *Sal didn't know yet*. That was why he was walking away. Not because he didn't care or because he didn't grasp the urgency of the situation, but because he absolutely *did* care and *did* grasp the urgency and was immediately trying to pull away to process all the factors.

Chart 6.1 (MEN): If you had to choose, how do you most instinctively want to process an emotional issue that affects your family or your job?	
I want to think it through internally, to figure out what I am thinking and feeling; then I feel like I can talk about it.	69%
I want to talk about it; that helps me think it through and process my thoughts and feelings.	31%
TOTAL	**100%**

Source: Decision Analyst Survey. Question/answer choices simplified.

Such as, were there really only two choices? What were the chances of the refrigerator being repairable? How much do fridge parts cost? How long would that last? Would the Johnsons have room in their chest freezer to store the party food until they bought a new one? And on and on.

Because Desiree didn't realize this was happening (because it was all internal!), she made it much harder for him to have space to process the very answers she was looking for. This might hit home with some of us (ahem).

One representative man described this frustrating feeling:

If we have a disagreement, I feel like I'm at such a disadvantage at the beginning because my wife is much quicker on her feet. She's marshalling all these thoughts

164

and arguments, and I can't even think. And I don't want to be a jerk about it, but the only way I'm going to figure it out is if she leaves me alone!

from
JEFF

🔒 **Women find it helpful to think something through by talking it through.**

Guys: By contrast, a woman's brain is wired for mental multitasking, including processing and talking about thoughts and feelings all at the same time. While that sounds exhausting to me, it's the way they are wired. Although plenty of women do default to processing internally (and all women can process that way if they need to), most women we interviewed described instinctively wanting to process *with* someone at times. One female attorney explained it this way:

> If a decision needs to be made and I'm unsure, I want to call someone. My husband or my sister. I usually say, "Give me your advice," but it helps even if I don't take their advice. If my sister suggests something, it's like my thoughts leap ahead and I start thinking about why that's a good or bad idea. Sure, I could go do research instead, or I could sit and think, or I could wait a day and come back to it—but all those things take time, and often all I need is a five-minute conversation.

Guys, when we hear things like this we may think it sounds illogical or even scatterbrained. Multiple men have privately said things like, "My wife is all over the place."

But here's what we absolutely must realize: She's *not* all over the place. *She's just doing on the outside what we do on the inside.*

That was what was happening in Desiree. She told us later that she wanted—*needed*—to talk through the options with Sal. Not just because she wanted to know what he was thinking, but also because she had no idea yet which was the right decision, and the act of conversation would help her process it.

Yet their conflicting processing styles left him feeling harangued and her feeling—as she talked to his departing back—as if he didn't care, didn't really understand the situation, or both.

Those were extremely common feelings among women. After all, guys: If we are processing something internally, by definition we are not talking about it. *Thus our wives have no way of knowing that we are processing.* To them, it looks the same as if we're ignoring them or the situation.

And it may get even worse after the processing.

Quite often, after a guy thinks things through carefully—weighing all the options and ramifications—he comes back and says, "I think we should do *this*." In his mind, it's settled.

But she thinks this is the *beginning* of the conversation!

This is the first she's heard of his decision, after all. So in order for her to process, she now needs to talk it through. ("What happens if the fridge dies overnight and

the food is ruined? Can we afford to get a caterer instead?")
This can easily cause yet another round of issues: He might
feel, *You don't trust me*; she might feel he is oversensitive
or trying to railroad her, and so on.

As you can imagine, it makes it much easier when we
expect our partner will need a certain type of processing
and understand what is going on when we see it, rather
than getting defensive. It helps when a man respects his
wife's need to talk things through, or a woman recognizes
that it will help her husband not feel criticized if she says,
"Okay, thanks for telling me that. Do you mind if I think
out loud about this for a minute?"

Surprising Truth #2: Our different processing styles require different amounts of time.

Whenever there is an issue that requires thought (as opposed to, say, "Which movie should we go to?"), we often
find ourselves at odds simply because our thought processes require different amounts of time.[42]

Perhaps because a woman's brain is wired with
so many connections within and between the hemispheres,[43] she appears to have a sort of instantaneous
surface-level processing of whatever money issue she's
thinking through. Not just immediate decisions like
the cranky refrigerator, but anything under the sun.
Should we invest the bonus or put it in a college savings account? Can we get by with a generic medicine,

or should we do the expensive name-brand one the doctor prescribed? How soon can we start rebuilding our creaky deck?

As each question goes into that interconnected computer network in her brain, she has an initial thought about it right away. Then she thinks it through more and more deeply as she talks about it, does a bit of research, ponders it, and perhaps talks about it some more. But the initial signals in her brain pass instantly, so she has an immediate starting point for what she's thinking.

As you can tell, the male brain doesn't necessarily work that way. On any issue that he believes requires thought—*especially* if there is marital controversy or emotions involved—the isolated supercomputers in his brain do their deep one-thing-at-a-time work, processing thoroughly. And that takes time.

Researcher and author Michael Gurian has extensively studied the neuroscience about boys and men. As he relays in *What Could He Be Thinking?*, neuroscientists have discovered, "Men can take up to *seven hours longer* than women to process complex emotive data." He notes, "Men more than women will not know what they feel at the moment of feeling and will take longer to figure it out. [And] men more than women may not be able to put their feelings into words at the moment and will tend to take longer to express feelings in words than women do."[44]

In practice that leads to several common scenarios.

Answering the next day

Seen this one before? A wife and husband are having a tiff at dinnertime. The wife asks, "What are you feeling about what I just said?" only to hear, "I don't know!" Then the next morning at breakfast, he's able to talk about it.

One man gave a good example of this time frame at work. "My wife was upset that I didn't want to let our thirteen-year-old son have the money to go to the amusement park with a friend—and that I couldn't really say *why* I didn't want to. The thing is, I want to say something the right way or it's going to get worse. If I say it wrong, it's going to blow up. The next day I sat down and said, 'Here's what it is: Our son has been no good at time management recently, and if he's gone all Saturday, how is he going to study for midterms? And I think he needs to see that these expensive days out are something he *earns* with a lot of diligence, and we haven't seen that yet.'"

Having to revisit agreements

And that raises a whole other issue: What happens if the husband *didn't* allow enough time, and agrees to something "too soon"?

Now, regardless of gender, many of us have experienced moments when we made a decision before we had a chance to truly think about it—and then realized afterward that there was a problem. But the men seemed particularly concerned about it. This could have happened because they felt pressure to move quickly or because they simply hadn't realized the complexity of the situation. Regardless, by the time they recognized they had a problem, their wife had been moving forward under the original decision. Understandably, this can cause issues!

Look at this scenario with a couple in their thirties, married two years, who we'll call Beth and Brent:

> *Beth:* I feel like we have an issue with communication, where maybe he is not always open and transparent. Brent is on the worship team at church and plays drums, and he has a lot of different drum sets. We decided to sell stuff we didn't need to gather a down payment to buy a house. I sold all the furniture I had in storage from my old apartment and put the money into savings. He sold a snare drum, but then bought a different drum. He said, "Oh by the way, I'm just getting this other drum, but I won't need any more after that." I was so upset. I stuck to our agreement and he went back on it.
>
> *Shaunti:* Brent, what was the situation from your perspective?
>
> *Brent:* The first thing I thought, when we talked about it, was that I was totally on board with selling stuff and putting money into savings. Yes, let's

do it. But a day or two later, I realized I first need to switch out what I have and get the *right* drum set so I *can* sell off all these other pieces.

Beth: Huh. But you never communicated that!

Brent: I need to be a better communicator. But, Beth, can I be honest? (She nods.) I might say "yeah, sure" and then think about something and want to change it, but when I try, you get mad and tell me that I'm going back on my agreement. I'm not going back on anything, I've just moved forward in my thinking. So I sort of feel that if I'm going to get in trouble either way, I might as well get in trouble after I've fixed the problem.

Beth: But then what do I do? I'm moving forward based on our agreement! It doesn't seem fair for you to say, "I didn't think it through."

Brent: Maybe we need a cooling-off period! You know, like, "Let's say we're doing *this*, but we have twenty-four hours to make changes before we start moving on it."

While the cooling-off period won't work for everything (here's looking at you, broken refrigerator), it might be a helpful idea that sets reasonable expectations in some cases. And it would allow *both* spouses to adjust things as necessary.

Surprising Truth #3: To aid our own processing, we sometimes do things that confuse or annoy our partner.

Often the way we handle *our* processing differences tends to make things more frustrating for our spouse. Once again, let's look at this from the men's and women's perspectives.

from SHAUNTI

Men: Too many variables getting in the way? Simplify—by shutting them down.

Ladies, because the male brain is wired to process one thing deeply at a time, men seem to feel that too many inputs or too many "extraneous" variables hinder their ability to process *anything*. Remember our discussion in chapter 4 about having open "windows" on the screens of our minds? In most cases, a man's ideal state is having one window open at a time. If there are too many factors to process, or too many things going on in the background, the guy feels as if there are a bunch of windows trying to pop up in his brain. Which can be really distracting.

Thus, for many men it is easier and more productive to radically simplify. To essentially say (subconsciously), "I don't want to think about anything else other than _____ right now."

We heard many examples of men doing this when faced with a money challenge. If he suddenly learned a big client might not come through, or was startled by a smaller-than-expected bank balance, he might make a decision that seemed arbitrary to his wife: "Let's not spend *any* more money for a while." Even if the thing he didn't want to pay for was already in the budget, or the cost was negligible, it would just make him feel better. This seems to be partly because of that "providing for the family" fear that looms in a man's mind, but also partly because it allows him to mentally simplify and focus on what he feels is most important.

I (Shaunti) see this at times with Jeff when we've had a few days of heavy spending—for example, back-to-school week, where we have to buy a ton of supplies or outfits all at once. Even if in the big picture we've planned for that spending, Jeff might say, "Let's not do our Costco run until next week, and let's not go to the movies this weekend after all. It will just make me feel better." Although no new income will come in between now and the later Costco run, it's a way he can mentally set aside the extra variables and uncertainty and not have to process them.

I have to recognize my reluctance to create a real budget adds to this. Especially since I also tend to handle the monthly bill paying, which means Jeff doesn't have context for what the big-picture financial situation actually looks like. That uncertainty in his mind is uncomfortable. So it feels better to simplify and close those uncertainty windows.

Will the honey-do projects get done?

A different application of this simplification is, believe it or not, honey-do projects. In many households, wives described their man agreeing to do a needed DIY project (replace the cracked glass in the kitchen cabinets, repaint the spackled guest room walls, etc.), but then feeling like the project just disappeared from his brain.

I (Shaunti) still remember when the main brackets and hanging rod collapsed in my closet and Jeff said he needed to rebuild all the shelves. I couldn't easily get to my clothes. Week after week, I asked Jeff if he was going to fix it, and he kept assuring me he would. *"BUT WHEN?"* I wanted to scream. "What's the holdup???"

Often, men described not doing a project right away because they simply had too many things on their mind. They needed to keep extra windows closed. Nearly all of them insisted that they do *not* forget about the project, but if they're busy, and if it doesn't have a deadline (if no visitors are coming to stay in the guest room that needs painting, for example), it becomes something they don't have to think about right now.

But because they process internally and often don't say things out loud, their wife has no idea! (As one woman rhetorically put it, "Did you forget about it? Do you not care? Am I going to have to do it instead because you won't?") Which means that similar to what we discussed in chapter 4, he has closed his window—and opened one for her.

This is also the main reason men and women have wildly different notions about whether the man needs reminders for honey-do projects.

On the Decision Analyst Survey, fully 78 percent of men said that when their wives asked them to do something (such as fix a broken cabinet), they needed either no reminders at all, or just one reminder within a week—and then their wives could completely let it go. But when we asked women the same thing, only 43 percent agreed. Perhaps the most shocking gap: 22 percent of the women expected their husband to not get the project done at all. They felt they would have to plan to do it themselves or get someone else to do it—whereas only 1 percent of men agreed. (Sign up to receive the full "Honey-Do" chart exclusively at thriveinloveandmoney.com.)

Most of these disconnects occur in whole or in part because she now has an open window—and he isn't talking about it. It makes all the difference if he will briefly share an update ("Just so you know, I haven't forgotten. I can't handle thinking about it right now, but I haven't forgotten"). Then, if it's important for her to get it done soon, perhaps she could propose a suggested deadline by which she will get someone else to tackle it if he hasn't.

In the Great Broken Closet Caper, I (Jeff) wasn't being lazy. A broken flimsy closet shelf could be repaired, but would inevitably come down again. I needed to gut and rebuild Shuanti's entire closet with a much stronger set of shelves. I'd never done this before, and I needed to figure out how. But I guess I never actually explained that. (In fact, Shaunti didn't learn that until we wrote this chapter!) All she saw was four weeks of not being able to easily get at her clothes.

She finally put her foot down (sweetly but directly), and asked me when I thought I would have it fixed. She then proposed that if I didn't get it done by then, she could hire a handyman to do it instead. I asked her to give me until the next Friday night. Well, wouldn't you know it, at 11:50 pm Friday I was up on a ladder rebuilding her closet shelving. Because now there was a (totally reasonable) deadline.

from JEFF

Women: Too many variables? Simplify—by thinking ahead.

Guys, let's switch this and look at how women handle processing all those windows at once. Although their minds can handle a lot of open windows, they don't like having so many things bother them any more than we do. But, as noted in chapter 4, since most women can't just decide to not think about something, they usually have to make an effort to close annoying windows.

For example, we heard from many women that when they are at a store, they are not only willing but eager to think ahead about things they might need in addition to the main item they went to buy. There are plenty of exceptions, of course, but this is why we heard many a confused (or annoyed) man wondering why his wife would pop into Target for a pack of batteries and come out with batteries *and* a bag of end-of-season clothes that would fit the kids next year.

I finally realized it wasn't a lack of self-control so much as a lack of time, and a desire to think ahead so she could close an open window. ("While I'm here, I might as well get . . .")

This same processing-variables-by-thinking-ahead dynamic comes out in an entirely different way via solving *potential* problems in advance. Again, we heard many examples of women who prioritized spending to address in advance a possible problem or need—allowing her to close a worry window. In her mind, that is well worth it even though that problem may not actually come up. Here's a helpful explanation from one woman:

> For me, the bulk of stress related to having a special-needs child falls on me, and I only have *this* much energy in a day.
>
> For instance, I personally care nothing for expensive hotels. I would backpack through Europe. But after hours in a car with a child who never stops talking, I need that downtime. If it was just for me, I'd be fine with a cheaper hotel. But I gain something by spending $20 extra to stay in a place with a nice breakfast instead of spending mental energy trying to figure out what restaurant in Oklahoma our son is going to be able to eat at. It is entirely about what I gain in time or sanity.

We may not always agree with our wife's reasoning, but understanding the variables will help.

And guys, sometimes it's not just a matter of understanding. Sometimes our role involves action to *help* her by eliminating time-sensitive or particularly troubling variables so she (and we!) can better process something. Think back to the refrigerator story. Sal wanted time to identify and think through all the options to get to the best one. But that time was painful for Desiree because of the uncertainty about whether she would lose all the food she had spent so much time preparing. Her thought processing kept landing on, *Whatever we do, we have to do fast, because of the party food.*

But imagine what would have happened if Sal had essentially bought himself the time he needed by solving her most crucial open window.

For example, he could have said, "Instead of running to Home Depot tonight, let's at least take care of the most important problem: how to make sure the party food is preserved. That's on me. I think we can find friends who have freezer space we can borrow for a few days. I'm going to call them right now."

Guys, notice: If something seems time-sensitive to our wives but we need the extra time, this means *we* need to take the responsibility to figure it out. It is showing great love and care for our wives when we take steps right away to close their most important open windows.

Surprising Truth #4: Our own way of listening can get analytical, but our partner needs engagement.

Guys, how many of you have heard a woman say, "I don't want you to fix my problem, I just want you to listen"? Well, it turns out that "listening" to a woman means something different than we think. Including when it comes to money issues.

But ladies, guess what? Don't be too critical. You may be gleefully ready to hear what we're about to tell your husband—and not realize that you do *the exact same thing to him that he does to you*, just in a different way.

> To communicate well about money, we not only have to understand the other person's processing style, we also have to understand how to *listen* in a way the other person needs.

If we're going to communicate well about money, we not only have to understand the other person's processing style, we also have to understand how to *listen* in a way the other person needs. It will take some practice, but the concept is simple:

from JEFF

Men, Listen to her feelings.

Guys, when our wife is bothered by something and processing it out loud, it may sound to us like she's going in circles. ("I'm so upset that Jeanne and Frisa aren't paying me back for that expensive dinner. And now they aren't talking to me! I didn't mean to offend them! But I had to say something, right? Or maybe I should have waited. . . .") Or it may seem logical that if she took a particular action, it would solve the problem and make her feel better. So we say, "Honey, here's what I suggest." But then we get the upset look or hear, "You're not listening to me!"

There is a lot more about this in *For Men Only*, but here's what's going on: Your wife isn't just verbally processing the problem. If she's like the vast majority of women, she's trying to process her *feelings* about the problem. She's all stirred up. Most women can't easily process their feelings on their own. So yes, she may indeed be talking in circles—because you aren't listening well! By focusing on solutions, *you keep short-circuiting her efforts to process her feelings!*

For most women, "Listen to me!" means doing these two things in order:

Step 1. "Listen to my *feelings* about the problem." Express empathy. Enter into how she's feeling as much as you can. Show her that you care. Ask questions to pull out *more* feelings than she's already expressed. ("I'm so sorry. What did Jeanne say when you asked her about paying you back? Did you think they were talking about it behind your back? Are you worried about seeing them at the office tomorrow?")

Step 2. "Help me think through a solution—if one is needed." After processing all those jangling feelings, you'll see her relax a bit. She'll feel heard. Then (and only then!), you can move on to discussing potential solutions—if those are still needed.

Chart 6.2 (WOMEN): Sometimes a woman will share something with her husband that she's concerned about. ("My boss really embarrassed me in front of the team today.") If you do that, what are you looking for?*

I am looking for input and analysis on how I can solve the problem.	**9%**
I am looking for my husband to just listen to how I am feeling.	**41%**
I am looking for him to listen to how I am feeling, and then I'd like his help solving the problem.	**44%**
I never share things like that anymore, because he would analyze/solve it instead of listening to how I am feeling.	**6%**
TOTAL	**100%**

Source: Decision Analyst Survey.
*Among women who indicate they say things like this.

On the Decision Analyst Survey, among women who share things like that with their husbands, 91 percent said this "listen to my feelings first" approach is what they are looking for (Chart 6.2).

Think back to the story of Sal and Desiree at the beginning of the chapter. When she said, "I'm really worried about this!" it was a subconscious appeal to her husband to listen to her feelings—in that case, her worries about having spent weeks preparing for her sister's big day, and now potentially having it all fall apart.

We guys may think, "Talking about the problem won't fix it." But in this case, listening and talking *will* fix something. It won't fix the refrigerator, but it will fix the fact that Desiree is worried and is feeling that her husband doesn't care.

Keep in mind, fake listening doesn't help! Here's an example of a man who just didn't get it:

> She is verbal. When she gets frustrated, she's not necessarily frustrated at me. But she has to talk it through. So I nod and smile, which she hates. She says I'm not really listening. But I'm just waiting for her to get to the point that I know she'll get to in a few minutes.

Gee, I can't imagine why his wife feels he isn't listening. How much better would it be, guys, if we developed the habit of actually helping them process their feelings?

Women, listen to his dreams.

Ladies, here's what we don't realize. Our men have something they deeply want us to listen to as well: their "blue-sky" dreams of the future. ("Wow, see that car over there? I think I'd really like to buy and fix up an old '65 Mustang at some point." "When the kids are out of the house, wouldn't it be fun to move to Maine and open a B&B?")

But because this usually involves money (and may sound crazy!), we often do exactly what we get annoyed at our husbands for: We get all analytical. ("Wait, what? You've never said anything about wanting to fix up old cars. Do you know how to do that? If that car was in the garage, would one of us have to park on the street? How long would it take . . . ?")

The thing is, in most cases, all our man is doing is dreaming out loud with the most important person in his life—and hoping we will dream with him.

It may seem surprising that men who process most things internally actually want to talk about their blue-sky dreams with their wives! But it says something about the way they feel about us, how vulnerable they're being when they talk through their big, crazy, fun ideas, and how much they want us to enter into the joy of dreaming together. ("Oh, that sounds like fun. I didn't know you were interested in restoring old cars! Does a '65 Mustang mean something special to you? Tell me about what got you thinking about this!") Among men on our Decision Analyst survey who said they shared this sort of thing with their wives, 76 percent indicated they want us to just dream with them and listen without analyzing.

A woman in a focus group shared a great example of how easy it can be to miss what our husband needs—and how we can enter into his dreams instead:

> Jimmy works for a bank but has always wanted to do more. He would say things like, "It would be fun to move to New York City and be a trader." Absolutely my first instinct was to say, "But there's no good schools, and how could we afford a place big enough for three little boys!?" I finally realized what he wanted me to say was, "That would be awesome. Let's totally do it!" I know his next step is not going to be, "Great, let's go buy a ticket!"
>
> I think some of it is a bid for affirmation. You know how we say, "Do I look cute in this outfit?" and we're angling to hear "You look awesome." His version is wanting to hear "Ooh, a trader? You totally have what it takes!"

I know what some of us are thinking: *Um, but what if his next step really is "Great, let's go buy a ticket!"?* Here's the best advice I received from a man when I asked that question:

> You have to trust him. He's not an idiot. Just because you're dreaming alongside him doesn't mean he's suddenly

184

going to set aside all reality. But if he really does have something he wants to do with his life someday, wouldn't you want to know that?

Yes, I'd love to sail around the world, but my kids need to be in school. And then my kids will have kids and I'll want to be around for them too. It's fanciful. But for my wife to enter into it and enjoy it with me is a shared pleasure.

Overall, it really is amusing that each of us wants our partner to listen by coming alongside without trying to analyze or fix—and yet neither of us tends to listen in a way we'd want to be listened to.

Top Tips

As we processed everything we listened to (see what we did there?), we realized there are several key actions that set us up for great communication. These steps will go a long way toward avoiding *other* problems that will need to be talked about!

Honor each other's processing styles.

Since the generalizations in this chapter will not apply to everyone, understand your spouse's processing style. Then honor it and work with it, rather than expecting your spouse to be able to process in a way that goes against how they were designed.

If you tend to fit into the gender patterns we described, here are a few specific ways to do that:

Women:

- If possible, give your man the time he needs to process without pushing.

- If needed, jointly agree on a time frame by which he will answer. And then let it go until then.

- Trust that he is thinking about it/planning to do it.

Men:

- If you need to go away and process, give your wife a time frame by which you will answer (e.g., "Give me until after dinner" or "Give me until Thursday").

- Realize that while you are processing—even if you've done the step above—the waiting time can be painful to your wife because her window is open.

- Expect that after you have processed and shared a decision, your wife will need to talk it through. Don't take it personally. She is now doing on the outside what you did on the inside.

- If possible, ask her what she is thinking about the matter *before* you go off to process for the first time. That way you're including her initial thoughts in your analysis.

- Don't be wed to your thoughts; be willing to process more if she raises ideas or factors you hadn't considered.

Then, remember what your spouse needs as you go.

Women: When your man finally shares what he's processed on his own, realize that in his mind he's likely sharing a fully formed decision, not just brainstorming. As you process his decision out loud, it can come across as criticism. So say, "I need to think out loud for a bit. I'm not criticizing your thought process; I'm just processing."

Men: Regularly make sure she knows you're thinking about something internally, especially if it is something she's waiting on. For example: "I want you to know that I *am* thinking about your closet, and I'm still planning to rebuild it by Friday."

Both: Once you've both had a chance to process, state out loud where you believe you've landed. Say, "Is this what we're agreeing to? Or do we need more time to consider it?"

On emotional issues, listen and enter in.

Men, listen to your wife's feelings. Draw them out. Resist the urge to discuss solutions until she's felt heard.

Women, listen to your husband's dreams. Enter into them. Resist the urge to analyze until you get the sense (later) that he's considering moving forward.

Ready, Set, Communicate

If we can work with how our spouses are wired, we can communicate based on a true understanding of the other person. And we can be ourselves rather than shying away out of fear of how our spouses will respond.

Here's what one husband told us:

> I think I've had a fear of rejection. It was a fear of how my wife would react to things I wanted to say. So sometimes, if I think there will be controversy, I'd rather keep the details inside, and not talk about them. On her side, I think she doesn't communicate sometimes because she thinks I will shut down. Or I won't really hear what she's saying.
>
> We've both been learning to be better communicators. It works better when we sort of pre-diagnose all those things we might have missed before, about what is going on in her or in me. I'm still not doing that perfectly. But here's the cool part: If you've already figured out how each other feels, and you care about each other, then there's nothing to fear from communication!

7 I'm Right, You're Wrong, What's the Problem?

How our knee-jerk reactions keep us from seeing the truth

Insight #5: We have knee-jerk reactions due to faulty beliefs about money or our partner.

We often started interviews by asking people to describe a situation in which they and their partner had either a conflict or a connection around money. Why did they feel the way they did?

Two trends quickly became apparent. First, most people had never thought about this question before. Second, as the person started pondering what was under the surface of their response, they nearly always began ruminating about their childhood. They felt a certain way because they grew up poor. Or rich. Or in a different culture. Or their parent was a certain way. As we dove deeper, those factors did appear to be part of the story.

But the more crucial part of the story—the more unrecognized and probably more important part—was *how the person reacted to those factors*. Sometimes their reactions seemed fairly average. But sometimes they described strong reactions—almost a knee-jerk, reflexive response.

We quickly noticed that those knee-jerk reactions weren't actually because of their background. A husband or wife might have very similar backgrounds but very different feelings and reactions. Even close siblings might have wildly different reactions to money—yet both claimed that their background was the reason they felt as they did.

One fifty-year-old woman I'll call Julie told us:

When I see my husband spend money on something frivolous, it makes me *so mad*. That's why we have two separate accounts. I'm a pretty strict saver because I had to take care of everyone from a young age. There were five kids in our family, and we didn't have a lot of money, but we had a great childhood. But then my dad was paralyzed in a car accident, and my mom died from an aneurism when I was fourteen. So I got a checking account and learned to drive. I'd take my brothers and sisters and go grocery shopping or to the laundromat. But we had almost no money. We didn't even have money for toilet paper, so Dad told us to use newspaper. So yeah, that's why I'm a saver. Because I never wanted my children to have to use newspaper as toilet paper.

But later in the interview when discussing a different topic, she said, "My older brother is completely nonchalant about money. He's like 'It will come. God will provide.' He thinks me being such a planner is irrational and annoying because we can't control everything."

It's not about the background.

What is actually underneath our knee-jerk reactions about money *isn't* our backgrounds, specifically, it's our *perceptions of how money "should" work*. That could be partially due to background and life experience, but also temperament, worldview, and other factors.

Without realizing it, Julie and her brother—like many married couples—are *operating on two different sets of strong beliefs*. In this case: "Things could fall apart at any moment; we need to set money aside!" versus "We'll be able to figure it out, it will be fine, and we can't plan the future anyway!" Neither is demonstrably right or wrong, but each is reacting under the faulty assumption that their own position is demonstrably right and the other person's is clearly wrong.

Thus, Julie is a compulsive saver, but her brother is compulsively nonchalant. (Who knew that was a thing?) And their knee-jerk reactions of irritation or anger are signals that a strong belief has been triggered.

We all do this to some degree. And sometimes those strong beliefs are based on thinking that is clearly inaccurate—all while each of us is convinced we are so obviously right.

> Both of us are thinking, *Why can't you see that you're wrong and I'm right?*

Of course, it is highly probable that our spouse has *different* faulty assumptions and reflexive reactions! We might plow forward in a certain way while our (puzzled) spouse seems passive or obstinate. Both of us are thinking, *Why can't you see that you're wrong and I'm right?*

Six Faulty Assumptions: Which Do You Have?

We define "faulty" thoughts about money as (a) those that a person believes are 100 percent true but are actually a matter of opinion, (b) those that a majority of objective observers would label as inaccurate, or (c) those that both relational science and biblical directives would label as unhealthy or damaging.

Although there are more faulty assumptions than we can list here, six categories were particularly common.

1. Expectations ("This is clearly the way things should work.")

2. Ownership ("The person who earns more money deserves more say/control.")
3. Fairness ("Money allocation should be fair; if you get this, I get that.")
4. FOMO—Fear of Missing Out ("If we don't do it now, we'll miss out!")
5. Projecting ("If you're doing X now, it means you'll do XX later!")
6. Motivations ("My spouse doesn't care.")

We should note that many other ways of thinking can cause knee-jerk reactions, but here we are focusing on those that stem from faulty assumptions. (For example, most outside observers would agree that a knee-jerk response might be appropriate if a couple agreed to spend only $10 each day on lunches, then the next day one spouse casually treated their entire department to a $300 lunch party.)

As you read, try to identify which perceptions might be in your heart. Diagnosing that is especially important to dealing well with some of the *other* issues we've tackled in this book. A knee-jerk, "this-is-so-obvious" reaction is a bit like locking the door on self-examination. It prevents us from going into other rooms in our minds and hearts, looking around, and trying to understand what we see there. It also prevents us from talking. After all, if my feelings and reactions seem so obviously right to me, what is there to talk about?

So let's open the door by briefly tackling each type of faulty assumption.

Category 1: Expectations
Faulty Assumption: "This is the way things should work."

Our history, family of origin, culture, temperament, personality, birth order, how we view our experiences . . . all these factors lead to expectations under the surface. We tend to assume, "This is just the way things should work," and often react reflexively. In our Dynata survey, 69 percent of respondents agreed that "My expectations for handling money are directly related to my feelings about how my parents handled money, or my experiences growing up" (Chart 7.1). We don't always recognize that this expectation isn't necessarily right or wrong—it's just *ours*.

Chart 7.1: "My expectations for handling money are directly related to my feelings about how my parents handled money, or my experiences growing up."	
Yes, definitely / somewhat	**69%**
No	**31%**
TOTAL	**100%**

Source: Dynata survey.

As noted earlier, these expectations about money can be extremely different even in close family members. (We even purposefully interviewed multiple sets of identical twins and found that most had different expectations and reactions to money.) Many of these expectations help explain why we value what we value (chapter 3).

This is important: The main reason we become unhappy or dissatisfied is that *we have expectations that aren't being met*. And since our partner often has different expectations, it is likely we'll *both* end up disappointed!

Here are some things we can have different beliefs, expectations, and reactions about. (Write down and discuss others that occur to you.)

Spending habits

One couple provided a great example of how different expectations and knee-jerk reactions interacted:

> *Her:* He was raised upper middle-class, and they tended to buy things if they wanted them. It worked out. But I grew up with a feeling of poverty. We only shopped at thrift stores and never ate out. And I see it come up in my reactions to things. I "nickel and dime" purchases and shop at thrift stores too.

Him: I want to give her things she won't buy for herself. Like save up and take her to the Apple store to buy her a new iPad.

Her: But we can get the knock-off, refurbished, three-year-old version. I simply can't go into a store and spend. I tried on a dress for our daughter's wedding and it looked gorgeous on me and it was almost $300! Absolutely no way.

Him: We had saved for that, and I tried so hard to get her to buy it, but she wouldn't. I wanted her to have the full experience of the wedding.

Her: There was one for $53 and I couldn't even do *that*. And the issue is, he'll spend on nice things that I do wish I had!

Getting out of debt

We spoke with one wife who felt strongly (often the sign of a knee-jerk reaction) that getting out of debt was very important. As she explained,

> Our highest priority should be to get out of debt, and stay out. We both like the idea of having a budget and being debt free. Well . . . Garrett says he likes it. We did a Dave Ramsey course, and candidly, I was hoping it would convince Garrett to see it my way about some spending differences. He went along with it and was willing to go to the classes and do various things, but realistically it was really just me rowing the boat.

This wife felt that *of course* being out of debt "should" be their highest priority. Her husband went along, but he wasn't passionate about it. He clearly didn't have the same expectation—and thus wasn't pulling on the oars in the same way.

Planning

Another common knee-jerk response is about the need for planning, or alternatively, the desire to *not* plan.

One woman told us, "My husband has this feeling that money will be there as needed, and that drives me nuts. He says, 'It'll come.' Really? How much will come?! He says we'll be able to figure the bills out—and we always have. But for me, I have *to know HOW* we're going to figure it out. Certainty is extremely important when it comes to money."

On the opposite side, one man said, "My dad planned and planned and saved for a great retirement with my mom. They didn't go out to eat, but by golly they were going to go on cruises in retirement. And then he died at sixty-six, before they went on a single cruise. Planning is overrated. We have a 401K and all that. But we also feel strongly we're going to enjoy our kids and our experiences along the way."

Both of those comments evidence both logic and knee-jerk reactions.

It is essential to recognize our personal expectations and call ourselves out on it. To recognize when our assumptions of how things "should" work are just that: assumptions. Preferences. And our partner's preferences may be just as legitimate. It is *particularly* important to recognize our reflexive reactions to money if they are hurting our relationships.

Think back to the wife who grew up with a feeling of poverty and had knee-jerk reactions against spending money. She explained how she finally came to terms with the fact that her expectations weren't necessarily correct. As she said,

> The day he tried to take me to the Apple store for the iPad and I was so snitty about it, I realized: I have to get over myself. I have to just say "thank you" when he wants to do something nice for me. Because it was making him sad and me resentful that he had these things and I didn't. And that wasn't fair to him. I still didn't get the $300 dress for the wedding. But I did agree to do a nice caterer and the touches that would make it beautiful. I was at risk of carrying that spirit of poverty into my daughter's life, and I didn't want that for her.

Category 2: Ownership
Faulty Assumption: "The person who earns more money deserves more say/more control."

Over and over again, in random coffee shop, airport and Uber ride interviews, we heard the phrase "Money is power" or "Money equals control." And some couples do have a straightforward struggle for control or independence (which we covered in chapter 5).

But as we dug deeper, we realized there were also crucial issues of ownership and entitlement under the surface. There can be a subconscious feeling (by either spouse) that the person who earns more money deserves more say. When this feeling is triggered, it can lead to extremely reflexive reactions.

"I deserve more say."

Many people believe quite straightforwardly that the person who earns the money should control it. On our Dynata survey, 40 percent of all respondents felt that way (Chart 7.2). These couples are more likely to separate finances to ensure each partner has control over "their" money. But many other couples strongly *disagree* with that concept philosophically, believing that to be one in marriage all funds should be equally owned, whether or not (for example) one spouse is a stay-at-home parent while another works full time. Which, according to the Department of Labor, is common: 30 percent of 25- to 64-year-old women earn little or no income.[45] (Very few men earn little or no income.)

The problem is, many people who say they don't agree with this sentiment actually live as if they do. This was the case for 71 percent of the sole breadwinners in our Dynata survey[46] (Chart 7.3). And many of these individuals have

199

the same knee-jerk reactions as those who more overtly agree with the ownership concept—even though they think they shouldn't.

Chart 7.2 Among survey-takers overall:

I feel that the person who contributes a lot should be able to have more say in how "their" money is spent. **40%**

Source: Dynata survey.

Chart 7.3 Among sole breadwinners:

I feel that the person who contributes a lot should be able to have more say in how "their" money is spent.

Yes, definitely/somewhat **48%**

I make significantly more than my partner, and I feel like they should respect that, when I have strong opinions on financial matters.

Yes, definitely/somewhat **71%**

Source: Dynata survey.

Look at this introspective, candid comment from a man who had built a prosperous business. His wife (at their mutual decision) had left the workforce twenty years earlier to be a full-time mom and support him in his business. This man seemed to be a good guy, had a strong faith, and believed (in theory) that all resources were jointly owned. Yet he confessed with chagrin,

It's not how she spends the money that bothers me. It's that deep down I probably feel the money is more mine than hers. That on some level I'm being philanthropic by giving it to her. Which is the age-old problem of a man suppressing a woman. Guilty as charged. It is a control thing. It stems from insecurity. I have to constantly check my insecurity at the door.

I often simply don't give what she is doing the same value. And yet Bethany is twice as capable as I am. But because of that feeling, I often hold her more accountable to her discretionary budget than I am to mine. She won't know I bought this extra fishing pole.

"I don't deserve as much say."

Of course, the ownership feeling works in reverse, too, with the spouse who *doesn't* earn as much money feeling that they don't have the right to speak up about how the money is spent. Which can be particularly damaging to the person—and to the relationship. As one stay-at-home mom described it, "I feel like I don't have much of a say. If he feels he wants to spend this or save that, what right do I have to overrule him when I'm not the one working for it?"

But, as many other interviewees pointed out, the non-income-earning spouse usually *is* working for it! They are doing what is necessary with the household, children, and often with the business, to ensure that the income-earning spouse is able to keep earning. Which particularly galls if they feel they are not being recognized for it. As one stay-at-home mom put it:

> When you are staying home and raising kids, that is working too. I'm choosing to give up money, a career, and opportunities, so our children can have a good life! You, my dear husband, get to go have business lunches while I'm changing diapers. And that is *fine* because we decided this together—but it stops being fine if I feel like I have to ask for money that should be mine just as much as yours.

I (Jeff) will confess to having had a version of this feeling. Shaunti's initial books and research began to take off not long after my technology company was forced to lay off all staff and close its doors. Thankfully, the book income eventually replaced the household income we lost. But I mentally began to think of that as "her" income, not mine, even though I was extremely involved in many of the projects. I felt like a second-class money citizen. Which is completely unfair, of course, since Shaunti has been very clear that she views all money as *both* of ours.

But let me (Shaunti) chime in here. It is true that I have told Jeff over and over that I view *all* income as equally ours. And I do. Yet I have also probably signaled something quite different by (for example) avoiding putting together a budget and thus avoiding accountability over how I spend money on things that *I* want (clothes, shoes, meals out . . .). If I'm painfully honest, I'm probably one of those who strongly *philosophically* believes that all money is "ours" while secretly feeling like I should be able to take some of the money "I earned" and spend it on a few things for myself.

"I need to keep control/I don't want control."

We should acknowledge that although a feeling of ownership (or lack thereof) appeared to be the most common reason one person exerted greater control over the money, another reason was because they felt their spouse didn't understand money as well as they did, or, conversely, because one person felt less than proficient with money and wanted their spouse to take over.

Nearly half of Decision Analyst survey respondents said they or their partner was either much better or much worse at budgeting, and as you'll remember from chapter 3 (Chart 3.1), nearly two-thirds on the Dynata survey felt they were better at managing money for the present *and* the future. Not surprisingly, some portion of people with those beliefs will act accordingly, and often this can lead to frustration and resentment.

There is such emotional freight that comes with feeling a lack of ownership over money. This leads back (yet again) to that "best practice" we saw among thriving couples: for each spouse (regardless of who earns the income or who feels most proficient at budgeting) to have an agreed-upon amount set aside each month that they could "own" and spend however they wanted without having to check in with each other.

203

Category 3: Fairness
Faulty Assumption: "Money allocation should be fair; if you get this, I get that."

If we have a limited bucket of dollars, we instinctively want that money allocated fairly. And if we feel those dollars *aren't* allocated fairly, many of us will set out to create fairness on our own, thank you very much.

And then, of course, we can define "fair" in a way that suits our own preferences.

Or perhaps we care more about the *process* being fair—that is certainly a high value for me (Jeff). I once heard someone describe themselves as a "high justice" sort of person, and realized that phrase describes me perfectly. I like rules to be equally applied. We saw several common ways this plays out.

"If you get this, I get that."

Even if we don't always act on it, we understand this feeling—including the envy that is often the trigger under the surface. As one woman put it, "I think to myself, 'Well, we're *supposed* to be cutting back on expenses, but you just spent $45 on a fantasy football tournament! So I get $45 for painting supplies.'"

Fully 40 percent on the Dynata survey felt a similar way (Chart 7.4).

We heard "it's the principle of the thing" too many times to count, and with vastly different examples—often

> **Chart 7.4 If you get this, I get that.**
>
> If my spouse/partner spends money to buy something
> or do something for themselves, I feel like I should
> be able to spend a similar amount of money for me.   **40%**
>
> Source: Dynata survey.

related not to the couple, but to spending money on extended family or friends.

For instance, a few months after a young couple, Steve and Nadine, moved from California to Pittsburgh, his parents offered to fly them back for a family wedding. A year later, five members of her family (of more modest means) wanted to come visit them in Pittsburgh. Because Steve and Nadine were more tech savvy and able to find better discounts, they offered to buy the $2,000 worth of tickets on their own credit card. But as the weeks and months went by, her parents and sisters weren't sending the promised reimbursement, and all parties grew more and more stressed. Then Nadine's mom broke down in tears; working at Winn-Dixie, she simply didn't have the money to pay for the tickets.

Nadine told Steve, "I don't want to be upset with my sisters or my parents. I know it's a lot, but what if we let it go, and just make this their Christmas gift?" To his credit, he eventually agreed.

But as Steve explained, "The problem was, I had to get over the differences in the dynamics of the families. After all, my family paid for us to come visit them! I found myself thinking, 'How much money are we giving to *your* family versus mine?' But I had to come to terms with the fact that 'fairness' doesn't necessarily mean 'exactly equal.'"

"I want it to be fair for you."

Most of us care about our spouses. But this leads to another common dynamic: We sometimes want to even things up for the sake of our spouse *even if* our spouse doesn't care about that!

As one wife told us, "He always insists on upgrading to the new phones. And he insists that I get one even if I tell him I don't need it! He always says, 'No, we both have to have it—it has to be fair.'"

Retaliatory spending

We can also have darker feelings—such as a desire to retaliate with our spending. As one woman said:

I find myself having this progression of not-very-nice thoughts. Like, "Oh, you went to McDonald's for the third time this week? We talked about saving on fast food! You obviously didn't hear a word I said. And now I'm feeling squashed and uncared-for, so I'm going to go out and spend money on Starbucks."

All that is crazy, because I know my husband cares about me! But I realize that's exactly how I get to that place in my thoughts.

Resentment

Sometimes knee-jerk feelings of resentment can be there even if we don't act on them. One woman described such a situation:

> David is *really* into basketball, and I'm not. He got a last-minute chance to go to the Final Four and watch from a friend's private box. It was an expensive ticket for us, but really a steal at only $75. But once he got there, he found out there had been a miscommunication: His portion was actually $300. He called me and was totally willing to come home, but of course I wasn't going to tell him no. But I was aggravated because money has been tight and we have expenses for the house. I was scrimping and working my butt off, and I found myself thinking, "He gets to spend money to have fun, but I don't get to do anything fun!"

Category 4: FOMO—Fear of Missing Out
Faulty Assumption: "If we don't do it now, we'll miss out."

Across all generations, all demographic groups, and both genders, we consistently heard about FOMO in ways that involve money. Things like, "If we don't do this vacation/class/experience now, we never will."

Of course, retail stores have known this forever. "60% off TODAY ONLY!" leads us to believe that "I *have* to make this purchase or I'm going to lose it."

In our Dynata survey, nearly eight out of ten people had FOMO with money, and seven in ten said they acted on it (Chart 7.5).

Chart 7.5: When there is a limited financial opportunity (such as very discounted airfare to a place we wanted to go, or a great sale on something we need), I have the feeling of wanting to grab it so we don't miss it.

Yes definitely/somewhat	**79%**
No	**21%**
TOTAL	**100%**

. . . and I usually do try to grab it

Yes definitely/somewhat	**70%**
No	**30%**
TOTAL	**100%**

Source: Dynata survey.

We observed several distinct types of faulty assumptions —all of which lead to the feeling that you have to do something *now*.

"I am/my child is never going to have the chance again!"

The options for this feeling are endless:

- The great sale at the store, the discounted package to Vegas, the cruise with your friends, the invitation your stepson received to join friends backstage at the concert
- The chance to eat as much as possible at this amazing restaurant *you're never going to be at again*!
- The suddenly open schedule that allows doing something with the kids/stepkids on the one day they don't have football practice or are not with your ex-spouse
- The celebration of your child's fifth/thirteenth/ sixteenth birthday or your friend's wedding/baby shower/next baby shower/retirement
- The chance to go on this vacation or have that experience before the kids come along/while the kids are young/before they leave home/while the grandkids are young . . .

Many of these are awesome opportunities that are worth seizing. The problem is that there are probably thousands of them!

"I have to do this while we have the money/before the money runs out."

Another faulty feeling that leads to knee-jerk actions is exemplified by this comment from a woman who grew up in a rural missionary family.

When we're getting close to the end of the month, I want to go buy something quick, while I still can. My husband is the reverse: He'll wait until we get the paycheck and then feel like he has more margin for stuff. But for me, when I know we're getting close to running out of money, I want to run out and spend. But then of course I feel guilty.

"This is a chance to beat the system."

We frequently saw people (more often men) wanting to grab a not-to-be-missed chance to "beat the system," "stick it to the man," or otherwise prove one's chops by grabbing a great deal. One man said,

Our yard requires sixty bales of pine straw. Each bale costs $6.50 through the neighborhood association, and they want you to only use their vendor. Then this other guy came knocking on doors and said he would charge $4 per bale and he'd even spread it. Sweet! Take that, neighborhood association! I gave him the cash and a few days later he comes back—and he and some kids are just throwing the bales over the side of the truck! I think I got 25 bales and I paid for 60. It totally backfired on me, so now I'm looking for the next deal to redeem myself.

That said, the *opposite* of FOMO can also lead to this same knee-jerk feeling. My (Jeff's) satisfaction comes from the reverse faulty assumption: I overrule that FOMO feeling and think, "Yes, my shoes have holes in them and that's a great sale price—but I'm not going to be manipulated by the system!" When I go back a few days later and those shoes are *still there* I feel like I'm in control. I bought them on my terms!

"I can't afford to not do this."

Many of us have the feeling that we can't *afford* to miss the chance to gain more money (think investments), more social connections, greater business advancement, more influence, stronger faith, or almost anything else. In reality, missing out doesn't usually cause irreparable harm—but it can be hard to believe that in the moment.

As one college student told me, "Almost any time I'm hanging out in public with people it's because of FOMO. Half the time I don't really want to be there, but I'm worried my friends will be better friends with each other than with me, so I have to stay in the mix. And it can get expensive, with money for coffee, or movies, or whatever."

I struck up a conversation on a rental car shuttle with one business owner who chuckled as he considered this topic. "That's actually why I'm here. I would much, much rather have stayed home and done a video meeting. But when I heard that certain other people would be here, I had no choice but to jump on a plane. Chances are, it will be a wasted trip. But I have to ensure I don't miss those moments."

211

Category 5: Projecting
Faulty Assumption: "If you're doing X now, it means you'll do XX later!"

This faulty perception is so sneaky most of us don't even realize it is there. In our minds, we blow up something (a spouse's decision, a situation, a money problem) into something far bigger than it is by assuming it predicts something down the road. We project into the future and have knee-jerk reactions based on what we are assuming will happen.

As one man said, "If I'm looking at what she bought, it isn't just about *this purchase*. In my mind, it is one of many. Shoes last week and pants today will mean new tops tomorrow. And clothes for the kids the week after."

One couple we interviewed was six weeks into a second marriage for both and blending a family of seven teens and young adults. They described two major frustrations they'd had over their first few weeks of marriage, and we realized both were instances of a reflexive negative reaction to a probably inaccurate projection.

Here was hers:

> I was a single mom for twelve years, and suddenly I'm having to run money decisions by him, even though I've already made up my mind that I want something. A few weeks before our wedding, I wanted new blinds. I'd already picked out the color and everything. Suddenly, he's telling me no!

So then my mind starts jumping a few steps ahead. I start thinking this is a preview of what's to come. I'm not going to be able to buy anything that I want. In my mind, I had him saying no to all these other things the poor guy didn't even have on the table yet! He tells me later that he was thinking we'd buy the blinds after we'd managed some of the wedding expenses. But all I thought at the time was, "He's going to be saying no to everything!"

Here's his:

She wanted to get carpet in her son's bedroom. I absolutely did not want that. I said let's get an area rug—carpet is expensive. She said we got a carpet for her daughter as soon as we moved in, why can't we do her son's room too? I had to leave the room because I was getting so upset but I couldn't figure out why.

I think it might be part of a dispute over handling her son. We have had problems with him, and I think it is wrong to reward his misbehavior. Is she going to constantly pamper him? Time to hold the line!

The problem is that when we assume, "Today it is this, and tomorrow it will be something else," our knee-jerk reaction will be to hold the line RIGHT NOW.

This leads to the last (but definitely not least) of the faulty assumptions in this chapter . . .

Category 6: Motivations
Faulty Assumption: "My spouse doesn't care."

As we said in chapter 5, the most important secret of the happiest marriages from our earlier research is the steadfast decision to believe the best of our spouse's intentions toward us, even when we are hurt.

The natural human tendency is to believe the worst. "My spouse did that hurtful thing on purpose." We've heard this subconscious belief come out in so many different ways:

- "She's playing games."

- "He wants to control me."

- "She doesn't care how hard I have to work for our money."

- "He'll tell me nothing is going on, but I know something is."

- "She's getting upset. Here we go again with the drama designed to make me give in."

- "She's happy because I do most of the work, and she gets to do most of the spending."

One man perfectly captured the main reason for knee-jerk reactions overall: "People tend to think negative things first and work from there."

But according to our earlier research, those "he/she doesn't care" beliefs are *nearly always incorrect*. The vast majority (more than 99 percent) of us deeply care about our spouses—and our spouses care about us! (Chart 7.6) In our study, this was overwhelmingly the case, even in the most difficult relationships. The most important factor, if we want to thrive in our relationship, is whether we *let ourselves believe it* when we're hurt. And believing that truth is life-changing.

Chart 7.6: Do you care about your spouse and want the best for them, even during painful times?	
Yes absolutely/sometimes	**99.29%**
These days, not really	**0.71%**
TOTAL	**100%**

Source: *The Surprising Secrets of Highly Happy Marriages*. Of the 1,261 people officially surveyed, only 9 people answered "not really."

So What Do We Do About It?

Here are a few simple action steps that will help you hold back your knee-jerk reactions and faulty assumptions:

Step 1: List what applies to you/your spouse.

Go through the faulty assumptions in this chapter and identify which apply to you. Pay special attention to any that either of you feel strongly about. Strong feelings are a good indicator of a reflexive reaction. Especially identify any areas where you and your spouse feel very differently. All this will help you watch out for those reactions going forward.

Step 2: The next time you are upset, anxious, or have a reflexive desire to think or do something a certain way, ask yourself why.

Based on her work studying emotions, Dr. Susan David, a Harvard Medical School psychology professor, cautions that "emotions are data, not directives."[47] We need to harness and examine the knee-jerk feelings that could otherwise drive us. (Which also means we can't just ignore strong feelings, or reflexively repress anything that is uncomfortable.)

Her research jives with what we have found. Namely, give yourself space between the experience of a feeling (e.g., anxiety about spending money on a wedding, irritation that your spouse is telling you not to buy blinds, a desire to grab that discounted package to Vegas) and your actions. Ask yourself some probing questions. (For example, why am I feeling a desire to grab that package? Is it true that this opportunity will never come my way again? And does that really matter?) Taking a moment to examine your feelings will not only allow you space, but will also help you understand yourself and/or your spouse better.

Step 3: Ask yourself: Even if your beliefs seem eminently reasonable, does that mean your spouse's way is wrong?

As you ask yourself whether your perceptions are true, you may determine: Yes, I stand by my original knee-jerk reaction. Maybe even to certain outside observers, $300 would seem like a crazy amount to spend on a dress for a daughter's wedding. Or maybe anyone would agree that it *isn't* fair that my wife wants to stop asking her family for the $2,000 they owe for the airline tickets.

But just because your own perception seems accurate and reasonable—does that mean your spouse's way is *wrong*? Don't misunderstand: We're not suggesting that truth is malleable, or that there's no such thing as right or wrong. But it is important to acknowledge to yourself and your spouse that sometimes there is no clear right or wrong *in a given situation*. It becomes a matter of opinion and judgment. Of what each person values most. That is when you must have grace and trust each other's intentions.

Step 4: Honor your spouse's feelings.

Ultimately, the goal of this chapter is to make you aware of your own knee-jerk tendencies and your spouse's—so you can stop reactions that might cause problems. Once you are aware, you can catch what is happening, nip the problem before it becomes big, explain what you were thinking, and apologize in a way that honors your spouse. This brings an opportunity for connection—and maybe even unity.

For example:

- "I really appreciate that you want me to enjoy our daughter's wedding day, and I will! But I can't justify the $300 dress—I don't think I would enjoy the day as much."

Or,

- "Sorry I flipped out about the blinds. I realize I'm projecting into the future again. I don't necessarily agree that we need to wait on the purchase, but I really appreciate your concern for the family."

Believe the Best, Let God Handle the Rest

Yes, that's a cliché. But there's a reason for clichés. Sometimes they work!

In the end, the most important way to confront false beliefs and knee-jerk reactions is to always trust God and believe the best of our spouses' intentions toward us. That trust is the best antidote. As we spoke with thriving couples in our research, over and over we heard comments like these:

During the hard years, we cried a lot about money, but we didn't argue. We didn't blame each other. We knew we had to let God handle the providing. We had to have each others' backs. The only thing that keeps me from insane worry is that we have seen God provide over and over again.

And,

I find myself sometimes thinking my wife doesn't appreciate what I'm trying to do to stay afloat. But underneath, I know that's not true. I force myself to remember all the ways she *is* doing what we need—how she makes me dinner every single night for my late shifts so I don't have to buy from the food truck. And when I'm willing to trust her and focus on the *truth*, there's no room for the false feelings.

8 The Best Return

How your investment in understanding will pay off

Remember our opening story of what I (Shaunti) thought, when we were first approached about doing this research? We didn't know if we wanted to tackle this topic of love and money because we were pretty sure it would change our lives.

It did.

What we have learned has challenged us as a couple. We were forced to confront the fact that even in a relationship that was wonderful in many ways, we weren't experiencing the true unity God designed for marriage. There was a giant part of life in which we each did our own thing, either stubbornly avoiding coming together (Shaunti) or checking out (Jeff) when it came to money. At times it was challenging to address money-related perceptions, habits, and preferences we had fought about or simply avoided.

Yet we would never go back.

Yes, we had to be willing to confront our own stuff. We eventually (gasp) *actually created a budget*. But as our understanding of ourselves and each other grew, it was as if we walked out of the cramped little room in which we had stubbornly been living, through a doorway and out onto a wide-open lawn with a beautiful view.

We were foolish to cling to that room. Leaving it behind was much less painful than we thought it would be. Why would we ever go back?

The Habits That Matter

Your love and money journey may be very different from ours. Maybe you've never clung to unhealthy habits and have communicated about money well from the beginning. Or perhaps money is just one in a list of things that cause marriage stress.

Whatever your situation, working to understand how and why you and your partner respond to money will improve *everything* in your marriage. Why? Because as we said at the outset, money gives us a window into the heart. You, too, will find yourself leaving behind that little cramped room and walking out into the sunshine.

That process does *not* have to be hard. And it will be even easier once we set aside the subconscious belief that if we just had more money, everything would be better. It's not true! Instead, there are a few key habits that truly *do* make everything better. Habits that will make it enjoyable instead of a chore. You—like us—may wonder why you waited this long.

Believe the best

We'll say it again: Believe the best of your spouse's intentions toward you. Your mate may have different opinions about money, drive you nuts, avoid things out of fear, or even dislike your way of doing something—but it doesn't mean they don't *care* about you and your preferences.

Whenever you're frustrated or hurt, get in the habit of telling yourself that your spouse *does* care (since that is almost certainly the truth), and look for a more generous explanation of their behavior.

For example, when your spouse is tense and asks if you two can review spending, instead of thinking, "My spouse is trying to control me," think, "I'll bet my spouse is worried because we had to dip into our emergency savings to fix the car, and he/she knows I'll need a new car soon."

Look for evidence that your spouse cares about you. You'll see it everywhere.

Cultivate contentment and gratitude

We all hope to be happy in marriage. But we can't *look* to marriage or money to make us happy; that's a recipe for a quick trip off the thriving path and into the swamp.

But what we *can* do is cultivate contentment—even gratitude. Contentment is a key component for happiness in any area of life—and absolutely essential for money and marriage.

The apostle Paul said contentment was a learned skill: "I have learned to be content whatever the circumstances."[48] And, "[I]f we have enough food and clothing, let us be content."[49]

> Contentment is a key component for happiness in any area of life—and absolutely essential for money and marriage.

One couple we interviewed, Fernando and Olivia, struck us as having an unusual level of contentment with their financial situation. They didn't have lots of money, but they displayed great respect and adoration for each other, and over time had become genuinely relaxed with the serious financial challenges they encountered. How did they do it?

Jeff: Have you always been like this?

Fernando: Definitely *not.* I've always been the person who worries about money. I would stress to the point of panic attacks. A few years back, I was going through a serious depression because of our finances. I'd go to church, but for some reason I started to really listen to what was being said. I talked to God, and I put it in His hands. It worked.

I make $18 an hour and we have a family of five in one of the most expensive cities in the country. Our rent alone is $1,900 a month. But we have working vehicles and our kids aren't deprived. Somehow, someway we make it happen. I work two jobs. And even with all of that, I know we're kind of broke.

Olivia: But we love our lives. Our three girls share one room and they don't complain. We have three twin beds in one bedroom. And two dogs and seven fish.

Fernando: And a turtle.

So how did Fernando and Olivia go from stressed out to contented?

Trust God Cares

It's a lot easier to be content and walk through difficult moments in your love and money journey when you trust that the Creator of the universe personally cares for you. You become grateful. Here's the rest of our interview with Fernando and Olivia:

Olivia: A few years back we were worried that our electricity was going to be cut off in two days. So, we're stressed to the max and Fernando was in tears. He said, "I can't do this anymore." Finally we said, we have to put it in God's hands. God is going to take care of it. Trust it will happen.

That was a big step. And then the next day we got a check in the mail for almost the exact amount of the overdue bill.

Fernando: We don't take that answer to prayer for granted! It was an eye-opener. Now, we just adjust our needs to what we can do.

Olivia: And somehow God provides.

Fernando and Olivia learned to trust God's care for them, and they learned to trust each other. Even though they had very different styles, not once in our long interview did we hear them complain about the other's approach to handling money.

Develop and recognize generosity

It is a paradox, but both scientists and students of Scripture know it works: If you want to thrive, be generous. Not just in money, but in everything surrounding it (time, effort, care . . .). As the ancient proverb rightly captures: "The generous will prosper; those who refresh others will themselves be refreshed."[50]

But also: *Recognize* generosity on the part of your spouse. This will come out in many ways, but we noticed a lot of couples mentioned the "generosity" of their spouse when flexibility or adjustments were needed. One man provided a good example:

We each have $400 per month to spend however we want. If I know she's already spent her monthly amount but there's something that costs $300 that she really wants, it gives me great joy to take $300 from my pot and give it to her. And conversely, if at the end of a month, she says to me, "I didn't spend $200 of my budget this month. Why don't we put it in savings?" that blows me away. She knows savings is a high value to me and she's choosing to do that for me instead of spending it on something for her.

We need to see generosity. And practice it. Because it detaches our hearts from our money.

Come together to create cushion

As we approach the end of this book, let's think back to the beginning. As we said in chapter 2, our efforts to understand one another are crucial for the two actions that will most lead to thriving in love and money: (1) being able to talk about money; and (2) having a financial cushion (regardless of your income level).

We have not discussed the technical aspects of how to build cushion. That was by design, as we felt there are already so many great books and tools available to help us manage our money or budget in effective ways.

But as we wrap up, it is important to emphasize that we can't *just* talk. We also have to *do*.

There are many avenues to building cushion and a decent financial foundation—so the key is to make that a goal and get started. But we did see that building cushion is more likely among couples who develop budgets and generally adhere to them (while permitting flexibility as the need arises). Having agreed-upon goals for your money can remove uncertainty and anxiety. And the act of doing so forces couples to come together!

On the Dynata survey, 78 percent of couples said that yes, money could cause issues between them—but there are ways it has also drawn them closer together. One survey-taker summarized how: "We have monthly meetings to go over the budget and have little trouble staying on the same page since starting this practice. It is no longer a large source of anxiety in our lives."

Another said, "In the talks we have, we are each other's support system. When money does get tight, we handle it together. . . . It's nice not facing the world alone."

The resources at thriveinloveandmoney.com, especially the *Thriving in Love and Money Discussion Guide*, are designed to get you started in a simple but effective way.

Have grace with each other

Very soon, it will happen. In the early stages of learning how to talk about money without wanting to poke your spouse in the eye, he or she will do or say something that seems crazy.

Have grace with each other. Sometimes, it's easier to forgive near-strangers than the ones we love most—but that is where we need to start.

Build flexibility into your expectations and guidelines. Yes, there are times when you need strict guardrails, such as if you're trying to claw your way back from a mountain of debt to get a mortgage, or breaking a habit of severe independence.

But in general, have grace. The budget is there to serve you, not you to serve the budget. Allow each other room to breathe. In the same way you would want your spouse to give you grace, give it to them.

Live in hope

Let's wrap up with this wise line from Andy Dufresne from the movie *The Shawshank Redemption*: "Hope is a good thing, perhaps the best of things." Andy went through many challenging—even brutal—things. But he kept his equilibrium and a good attitude because he maintained his hope for the future.

You can too.

Today, the two of us have a budget. We can talk about money. Shaunti understands why she can get defensive or is tempted to hide purchases, and chooses to be open instead. Jeff catches his tendency to check out, react out of fear, or think the book income isn't really "his." We know where the other is coming from.

We still think the other person is nuts sometimes. We certainly don't always agree. But most of the time, we *understand*.

Acknowledgments

This book and this research is the result of thousands of hours of effort and input from hundreds of people. We cannot name all of you, but you have our deep thanks. Our special gratitude goes to:

The thousands of people who took surveys and shared their thoughts. Those who shared specialized knowledge, including Steve Caton and Chris Willard at Generis, Ron Blue, Todd McMichen at Lifeway Generosity, Michael Gurian, Kim Anderson, and several generous neuroscientists. Those who helped arrange crucial initial surveys and encouragement, including pastors Jeff Norris, Garrett Moore, and Kipper Tabb; and Beau and Nicole Hummel, whom we love and appreciate even though you root for OSU. The many who reviewed the initial book drafts in detail, especially Kerry Dodd and Gregg and Josie Pawlowski.

The survey firm professionals who ensured the surveys were fielded and monitored well for high-quality samples, especially Mauricia Wills at Decision Analyst, Michele Frisella and Kin Parikh at Dynata, and the original SSI team.

The amazing people who helped arrange all the formal research trips and shared so much wisdom and guidance, including Steve Carter, Tim Hester, and Jennifer Ballengee at Southeast Christian Church in Louisville, Kentucky. Our special thanks to Pastor Steve for your incredible insight and guidance at so many points along the way. Carrie and Greg Abbott, Crista Media and KCIS in Seattle, Washington. Julie Baumgardner and the team at First Things First. Robin Clay in Fredericksburg, Virginia. Teresa Shaw, Michele Koppmann, Pam McClatchey in El Paso, Texas. Faith Lawler and Fred Wilson in Atlanta. Margarita Robinson, Courtney Young, Jeremy Sukup, at The Rock Church in San Diego, California—and Pastor Miles McPherson for your great encouragement.

The tremendous professionals and friends at Thrivent and the original Love & Money Project, including Nikki Sorum, Jan Engkasser, Laura Dierke, Callie Briese, Zach Snell, Tim Wyngaard, and Suzanne Olson; as well as Mary Messina for hours of Zoom partnership and sisterhood, Rafa Robert for your leadership, Andy Langenfeld, Danelle Rymsza, Ann Lindquist, and the rest of the original Love & Money team: What you built has had a great impact—and will continue to.

The team at GLOO, expecially Scott Beck, Nancy Smith, and Drew MacMillan; FamilyLife, especially Brian

Goins; and Russ Crossan at Ronald Blue Trust for your partnership in the application of these findings.

The amazing people at Bethany House and Baker Publishing for your skill, patience, and prayer through the delays following my father's stroke. Special thanks to our astoundingly skilled editors Andy McGuire and Sharon Hodge, and to Deirdre Thompson and Rod Jantzen. Thanks also to our friend Lucy Iloenyosi at NeatWorks, Inc., for another cover home run.

Our amazing research consultant and literary agent, Calvin Edwards, and Nerida Edwards, for more than twenty years of unparalleled insight. We are so grateful for our friendship—and for that unexpected meeting at Ronald Blue & Company so many years ago.

Our survey design consultant/Research Jedi Master Dr. Charles Cowan, founder of Analytic Focus, for your generosity and skill over so many years, as well as Adrian Cowan, and also Sonali Saxena at Analytic Focus.

Our amazing internal team: We don't have words to properly express our gratitude for you all, especially Charlyn Elliott for your leadership and crazy ability to crunch any spreadsheet—you are the unsung hero in this project; Caroline Niziol, for juggling so many survey complexities and your mad social media skills; Tally Whitehead, for your incredible research talents and willingness to drive to a research library in a blizzard. Also, Naomi Duncan for adding great analysis into an already-full speaking management and church leadership schedule; Eileen Kirkland for your event skills and "I'm on it" willingness to do whatever needs to be done; Katie Phillips for running the editing team and process, and your sweet friendship over the years; Theresa Colquitt for jumping back into the fray and organizing so many research trips; Melinda Verdesca and Suzanne Stewman for your insightful analysis at just the right time; Deanna Hamilton for your young families survey analysis; and Greg Elliott for arranging a focus group and generous time in solving so many thorny spreadsheet problems.

The seventy-five dedicated people on our prayer team over the last three years; you have done the real work. You have sought God and prayed us through so many challenges. We are forever indebted.

Our family; we love you so much. We are so grateful for the Feldhahn clan, especially Gary, John, and Pat for your interest and encouragement, and for Jeff's sweet mom and dad who both went to be with Jesus during this process. We are especially grateful for the support of the Reidinger clan, including Rick and Canny for your input and encouragement, and especially to Shaunti's mom and dad. Mom, your bighearted willingness to host staff meetings, cook dinners, pick up whatever food was fueling our writing that week, and drive Luke home from school every day has made all the difference in getting this book done.

We especially want to tell our amazing children, Morgen and Luke, thanks for encouraging us and for your grace with the many days we were distracted. Despite the fact that your mom and dad didn't quite have their money act together, the two of you have grown into a young woman and man who don't feel entitled, and know the value of a buck. We are most grateful that *you* are grateful, and that you are living out your faith in Jesus every day.

Finally, to the Creator of hope; we would never have thought to research this love and money topic, but we're grateful you brought us to it. We are so thankful that you light the darkness, provide for those in need, and take every hard and difficult circumstance and make all things new.

A Love and Money Conversation Model

Your goal now is to talk about money *in order to* better understand each other, connect, and be on the same team. If you can do that without too much difficulty, go for it! But if talking about money has previously triggered anger or avoidance, we want to help you avoid those patterns now. It's time for a new, positive pattern. (And, if needed, please enlist a coach or counselor to help you create the best patterns for you.)

Below is a simple model you can use whenever a disconnect causes emotions to rise. Commit to each other that you will (1) follow the ground rules and template, and (2) believe that your partner cares about you and does not want to hurt you. Also, if the conversation starts to get heated, it's okay to take a break. Part of building healthy patterns is being able to table a topic and come back to it when you're able to respond well.

Ground Rules

When talking about a particular issue, one of you begins as the "speaker" and the other as the "listener." Talk through the template below. Then switch roles so each of you has a chance to speak and to listen.

Note: When the *speaker* has the floor, it is their turn to share their heart. The *listener* gives their undivided attention (no playing with a cell phone!), listening for the message the speaker is sharing rather than preparing to reply or to point out their own perspective. (If you are the listener, you *can* confirm that you are understanding a key point by repeating it back or summarizing it.)

Template for Talking

If you identify an issue that causes emotions to rise, complete these five statements.

1. **"On this issue, I feel _____."** (Or, **"The story I'm telling myself is _____."**)

   - This is *not* right or wrong, but identifying what we really feel. Example: "The story I'm telling myself is that you don't care that I have to work so much overtime to make up for your desire to eat your lunches out."

2. "Yet you must feel _____. Did I get that right?"

  - We try to put ourselves in the other person's shoes, then ask if we are correct. Example: "You must feel like you also work hard, and then I shoot down the spending that matters to you—like eating out. You feel like you deserve to eat out daily. Is that right?"

3. (Listener gives a very short reply) "Yes, that is generally it," or "Sort of, but let me clarify _____," or "Not really. It is actually that I feel _____."

  - The listener does not become the speaker but simply gives the speaker a basic yes/no answer (a few sentences at the most). More details can be shared during their own turn to speak. Example: "Kind of. It is more that getting out for lunch is my only real relaxation in a stressful job. I feel like I need that to avoid going crazy."

4. "Your concerns matter to me, too. Would it work for us to try _____?"

  - Brainstorm possible solutions, acknowledging how *both* of you feel. Example: "I don't want you to feel like you can't get that downtime, and I don't want to feel trapped. Would it work for us to set aside a pot of money you can use for

239

roughly *four* days a week out? But to do that, we would need to create a real budget."

5. **"If so, what are some specific steps that would get us there? Maybe _____?"**

• Suggest one or two short-term, tangible action steps. Example: "Maybe by next Saturday we could enter our expenses into an app or software package, so we know where our spending goes each month. And in the meantime, you could add up the total amount you can live with for eating lunches out four days a week."

After the speaker talks through this template, switch. Now the listener becomes the speaker and walks through these same statements. Make sure you write down your decisions and specific action steps!

NOTE: Find more help, including the *Thriving in Love and Money Discussion Guide*, at thriveinloveandmoney.com.

Appendix 1

Methodology: How We Did the Research

By Dr. Charles Cowan, founder of Analytic Focus

This chapter is published online at www.shaunti.com/research.

Appendix 2

A First Look at What Most Prevents Money Tensions

By Dr. Charles Cowan, founder of Analytic Focus

This chapter is published online at
www.shaunti.com/research.

Notes

Chapter 1: It's Not About the Money

1. Where necessary for clarity and presentation here, survey question/answer wording has been edited and data summarized, without changing anything material to the direction or findings of the original text or data. You can see the complete, unedited survey findings at www.shaunti.com/research.

2. Names and identifying details have been changed to protect anonymity. Interviews/quotes have been edited for clarity and length.

3. For a helpful article on this, see "Denying the Neuroscience of Sex Differences" by eminent neuroscientist Dr. Larry Cahill in *Quillette*, March 29, 2019, https://quillette.com/2019/03/29/denying-the-neuroscience-of-sex-differences/.

Chapter 2: A Daily Problem, a Simple Solution

4. S.M. Stanley and L.A. Einhorn, "Hitting Pay Dirt: Comment on 'Money: a Therapeutic Tool for Couples Therapy,'" *Family Process* 46, no. 3 (September 2007): 294.

5. Each survey found slightly different numbers, but the magnitude of tension and actual fighting was similar overall.

6. The young families survey was structured to allow greater understanding, care, and time for survey-taking, making it the best survey for in-depth points of tension analysis. Dr. Cowan conducted a meta-analysis

and found the young families survey results on the points of tension were a good representation of the results from all other surveys.

7. See, for example, C.G. Gudmunson et al., "Linking Financial Strain to Marital Instability: Examining the Roles of Emotional Distress and Marital Interaction," *Journal of Family and Economic Issues* 28 no. 3 (September 2007): 357–376, and K.L. Archuleta et al., "Financial Satisfaction and Financial Stressors in Marital Satisfaction," *Psychological Reports* 108, no. 2 (April 2011): 563–576.

8. Dr. Britt's study "Examining the Relationship Between Financial Issues and Divorce" concluded that financial disagreements were the leading predictor of divorce. However, the data set had some significant limitations, focusing on a narrow and very high-risk group (Wisconsin baby boomers getting divorced in a massive wave just as no-fault divorce was legalized) who were surveyed several decades ago (in 1987–1988 and 1992–1994). (See J. Dew, S.L. Britt, and S.J. Huston, "Examining the Relationship Between Financial Issues and Divorce," *Family Relations* 61, no. 4 [September 2012]: 615–628, https://doi.org/10.1111/j.1741 -3729.2012.00715.x.) Other studies have not found finances as *the* main reason for divorce, but certainly one of the key stressors for marriages.

9. Following the specific regression analysis to determine correlation, these two unranked tensions were identified as material and added to the list.

10. In our Dynata survey (unadjusted), those who said they could talk about money as needed were much more likely to be happy in their finances (no matter their income level): 55 percent were generally happy with their finances and feeling a sense of "lightness." Among those who talked with difficulty, or not at all, only 34 percent were generally happy with their finances in that way.

11. See the Appendix by Dr. Cowan, with a helpful, simple explanation of the statistical analysis of these factors.

12. For example, see J.P. Dew, "The Association Between Consumer Debt and the Likelihood of Divorce," *Journal of Family and Economic Issues* 32, no. 4 (December 2011): 554–565. The authors note, "Income was not associated with divorce in this sample. . . . The lack of findings for income may also support the idea often found in popular family finance books that income is not the biggest problem for families, but

rather it is what families do with their income that makes the difference (Poduska 1995) (p. 563)."

13. At least for a financial life that involves both spouses. Alternatively, one spouse could either check out or steamroll their partner; neither will result in thriving.

14. There is a range of comfort or awkwardness in talking about money. But in general, as Dr. Cowan summarized in his online Appendix "A First Look at What Most Prevents Money Tensions," "The more trouble discussing money, the more likely aggressive feelings and anger will exist and dominate."

15. See the survey portal on shaunti.com/research for how we reclassified these answers. (Part of best-practice for all survey analysis is cross-checking results to catch inconsistencies—especially revealing ones like these.)

16. Adjusted for greater accuracy, based on a conservative analysis of respondents' other survey answers. Based on clear statements of fighting or avoidance elsewhere, 350 people were moved from answer choice 1 to 2 or 3, and 12 people moved from answer choice 4 to 3.

17. Susan Cain, "How to Overcome Fear and Embrace Creativity," interview by Tim Ferriss, *The Tim Ferriss Show* (podcast), January 24, 2019. Cain is the author of *Quiet: The Power of Introverts in a World That Can't Stop Talking.*

Chapter 3: Can't Buy Me Love

18. Due to rounding, totals slightly exceed 100 percent.

19. Participants in the main Dynata survey were 27 percent more likely, and those on the smaller SSI survey were a stunning 82 percent more likely.

20. Dr. Curt Thompson, "With All Your Mind," interviewed by Arthur Brooks, *The Arthur Brooks Show* (podcast), March 21, 2019. The topic was unrelated to money, but the point applies to anything we have feelings about.

Chapter 4: Things That Go Bump in the Night

21. Although our research included input from everyone, these particular categories will therefore apply to heterosexual relationships;

the gender-specific knowledge is also useful purely for understanding ourselves.

22. The SSI survey was smaller, but because the makeup of a sub-group of female respondents skewed the Dynata results slightly on this question (and since the trends were otherwise the same), we are presenting the SSI data here instead. (Dynata data can be seen at shaunti .com/research.)

23. The primary exception to this was, often, women who had spent time as single moms.

24. The complexity of this concept made it impossible to assess using our online survey format. Thus, we quantified this factor via polls at events where we could explain the concept, and by categorizing feed-back from interviews. Consistently, roughly three out of four women (including women who describe themselves as "savers") were willing to spend money to put a distracting concern to rest (assuming it was a matter where money would help), whereas their husbands/boyfriends were far less likely to do so.

25. See endnote on Chart 4.6. Consistently, roughly two-thirds of men said it felt as if her action of spending money to close an open window had opened one for him.

26. This is also very foundational beyond money. More specifics and "what to do" can be found in our other relationship books (in particular, *For Women Only*, *For Men Only*, *The Surprising Secrets of Highly Happy Marriages*, and *The Kindness Challenge*).

Chapter 5: Show Me the Money—and Then Let Me Handle It

27. For details on how marriages were categorized, see *The Surprising Secrets of Highly Happy Marriages* and the shaunti.com/research portal.

28. Matthew 6:21.

29. See Dr. Cowan and Sonali Saxena's regression analysis in the survey portal at shaunti.com/research.

30. Percentage of those who acknowledged at least three significant actions or attitudes that avoid being one (hiding purchases, separating bank accounts, feeling like "it's my money," and so on).

31. Quote published in *The Surprising Secrets of Highly Happy Marriages*.

32. For example, see Dr. Cowan and Sonali Saxena's regression analysis in the survey portal at shaunti.com/research.

33. 1 Corinthians 10:31.

Chapter 6: What We Have Here Is a Failure to Communicate

34. The neuroscience in this chapter is drawn from many sources, including books such as *Why Gender Matters* by Leonard Sax, *What Could He Be Thinking?* by Michael Gurian, and *The Female Brain* and *The Male Brain* by Louann Brizendine; crucial research journal and other articles by neuroscientists such as Dr. Larry Cahill, including "Equal ≠ the Same: Sex Differences in the Human Brain" in *Cerebrum*; dozens of studies by neuroscientists between 1995 and 2019; a May 1, 2019, interview with Michael Gurian; and several off-record email and telephone interviews with neuroscientists. This is our best effort (as non-neuroscientists!) to synthesize input from many sources who may not always agree with or even be aware of each other's findings or resources.

35. M.D. Wheelock et al., "Sex Differences in Functional Connectivity During Fetal Brain Development," *Developmental Cognitive Neuroscience* 36 (Spring 2019): 100632, www.sciencedirect.com/science/article/pii/S1878929318301245#bbib0225.

36. Institute of Medicine, *Exploring the Biological Contributions to Human Health: Does Sex Matter?* (Washington, DC: National Academies Press, 2001), https://doi.org/10.17226/10028.

37. Although one could say that both gray and white are computing matter, gray matter is made up of the dendrites that bring in information and the cell bodies that control the function of the cell, while white matter is made of axons that connect different parts of gray matter to each other.

38. The specifics about men having more gray matter and women more white matter come from Michael Gurian, *Saving Our Sons: A New Path for Raising Healthy and Resilient Boys* (Spokane, WA: Gurian Institute, 2017), Kindle. However, note that different neuroscientists have different findings on this. The Ingalhalikar study referenced in endnote 39, for example, has a nuanced finding of more gray matter in the *female* brain. The science is not settled.

39. Madhura Ingalhalikar et al., "Sex Differences in the Structural Connectome of the Human Brain," *PNAS (USA)* 111, no. 2 (January 2014): 823–828.

40. G. Gong and A. Evans, "Brain Connectivity: Gender Makes a Difference," *The Neuroscientist* (2011), 17, 575–591. Also see R.C. Gur et al., "Sex Differences in Brain Gray and White Matter in Healthy Young Adults: Correlations with Cognitive Performance," *Journal of Neuroscience* 19, no. 10 (May 1999): 4065–4072.

41. Ingalhalikar, "Sex Differences." "Overall, the results suggest that male brains are structured to facilitate connectivity between perception and coordinated action, whereas female brains are designed to facilitate communication between analytical and intuitive processing modes."

42. Again, the information here is simplified, but is a reasonable interpretation based on the available neuroscience.

43. Larry Cahill, "Fundamental Sex Difference in Human Brain Architecture," *PNAS* 111, no. 2 (January 2014): 577–578, www.pnas.org/cgi/doi/10.1073/pnas.1320954111. Also see Larry Cahill, "Equal ≠ the Same: Sex Differences in the Human Brain," *Cerebrum* (April 2014): 4–5.

44. Michael Gurian, *What Could He Be Thinking? How a Man's Mind Really Works* (New York: Macmillan, 2004), 86. (Also see C. Hamilton, *Cognition and Sex Differences* [Basingstoke, UK: Palgrave Macmillan, 2008], quoted in G. Gong et al., "Brain Connectivity: Gender Makes a Difference," *The Neuroscientist* 17, no. 5 [April 2011]. 575–591.)

Chapter 7: I'm Right, You're Wrong, What's the Problem?

45. Department of Labor, "Labor Force Participation Rate by Age and Sex," 2016. Gender- and age-specific statistics can be generated at https://www.dol.gov/wb/stats/NEWSTATS/latest/laborforce.htm#LFPagesex.

46. On the Dynata survey, only 48 percent of sole breadwinners said that "the person who contributes a lot should have more say." Yet when given an example of having a "strong opinion" ("I make significantly more than my partner, and I feel like they should respect that, when I have strong opinions on financial matters"), 71 percent agreed—a 48 percent increase. Since "strong opinions" are present in many disagreements and passion tends to only come when there *are*

strong opinions, what those individuals are actually saying is that they secretly/subconsciously do agree with the first question.

47. Susan David, "How to Harness Your Emotions to Make Wiser Business Decisions," interview by Donald Miller, *Building a Storybrand with Donald Miller* (podcast), May 6, 2019. Dr. Susan David is the author of *Emotional Agility*.

Chapter 8: The Best Return

48. Philippians 4:11.
49. 1 Timothy 6:8 NLT.
50. Proverbs 11:25 NLT.

Go Beyond the Book!

Easily apply what you've learned, identify what you most need, or lead others to do so.

Visit our website for

- videos
- discussion guides
- assessments
- financial tools
- survey links
- discount offers
- leaders' guides

and more @
thriveinloveandmoney.com

Discover the Truth
He *Wants* You to Know

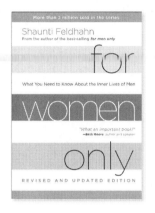

For Women Only offers fascinating insights into the hidden lives of men. Based upon a landmark nationwide poll, Shaunti Feldhahn offers groundbreaking information and advises how to convert her findings into practical application.

Finally.
You *Can* Understand Her

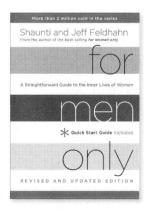

What makes her tick? What is she really asking (but not actually saying)? Take the guesswork out of trying to please your wife or girlfriend and begin loving her in the way she needs. Easily. *For Men Only* is a straightforward map that will lead you straight into her heart.

Read an excerpt from this book and more at
www.WaterBrookMultnomah.com